CHRISTIAN REALITY & APPEARANCE

JOHN A. MACKAY

Christian Reality

&

Appearance

JOHN KNOX PRESS
Richmond, Virginia

Standard Book Number: 8042-0510-8
Library of Congress Catalog Card Number: 69-19474
© M. E. Bratcher 1969
Printed in the United States of America

FOREWORD

The Alumni Association and Board of Trustees of the Austin Presbyterian Theolgical Seminary established a lectureship in 1945 to bring to the campus some distinguished scholar each year to address an annual midwinter convocation of ministers and students on some phase of Christian thought.

In 1950, the Thomas White Currie Bible Class of Highland Park Presbyterian Church, Dallas, Texas, undertook the maintenance of this lectureship in memory of the late Dr. Thomas White Currie, founder of the class and president of the seminary from 1921 to 1943.

The Currie Lecturer in 1952 was John A. Mackay, then President of Princeton Theological Seminary. The basic thesis of his lectures has become increasingly relevant, and in this volume Dr. Mackay develops it in terms of our contemporary situation.

DAVID L. STITT
President

Austin Presbyterian Theological Seminary
Austin, Texas

CONTENTS

PREFACE

Reality has been through the ages a major theme of thought and an unceasing quest of life in both the Occident and the Orient, in the secular order and in the religious order. What constitutes the real? Where is the real to be found? How is it to be defined? In what manner should it be lived?

For him who writes these lines, this question has been a deep concern from early youth to these sunset years. As a philosophy student at Aberdeen University, and in the wake of an experience of revolutionary inward change whereby Jesus Christ became the center of my being, I became fascinated by the title and substance of a book called *Appearance and Reality*, by an English philosopher, F. H. Bradley. "Metaphysics," said Bradley in this bulky tome, "is the finding of bad reasons for what one believes upon instinct. But to find these reasons is no less an instinct." The words gripped me.

Fifteen years later, as the incumbent of the Chair of Metaphysics in the western hemisphere's oldest center of higher learning, the University of San Marcos, Lima, Peru, I wrestled with the intellectual ultimates involved in Bradley's book and thesis. In a highly secular and sophisticated academic environment, I sought to evolve a Christian metaphysic. My class lectures concluded with a discussion of the Absolute, the reality of God, and the significance of that reality for the life of man.

Many years have passed, and phenomenal changes have taken place since the Victorian era when Bradley wrote *Appearance and Reality*. But the changing times and an emergent new mood give significant contemporary relevance to some of his basic contentions.

Bradley emphasizes the fact that the discovery and discussion of first principles is a prime necessity. For man is so constituted that he craves to comprehend what lies beyond the purely positivistic and empirical. The changed mind of each generation requires not only a new poetry but a new philosophy. Why? Because there is in human life a mystical dimension that is deeper and more complex than the rational and which renders imperative the cultivation of both philosophy and religion in the pursuit of true existence.

Reality, according to Bradley, while itself inscrutable, is no mere abstract absolute. It gives birth to diverse values. It creates standards which are an ultimate necessity for the shaping of man's life and relations. As regards religion, its source is the fear, or perhaps the admiration and approval, of some object that stirs absolute devotion. As for philosophy, its foundation is not a premise provided by reason, but an "instinct" or, as the term may be paraphrased, a sentiment, a concern, an experience, a revolt, a prejudice. That is to say, feeling in some form or another is the source of both religion and philosophy.

The basic insight of this Oxford don, who devoted his entire life to philosophical research, is of crucial importance. It has a decisive contribution to make to an understanding of why persons are what they are and act as they do, whether they be hippies or drug addicts, revolutionary students or uncommitted professors, anti-God theologians or concerned evangelicals. Reason is ultimately the servant of feeling, and everything depends upon the nature and the source of feeling. "The heart has its reasons which Reason does not know," said that philosopher-saint, Blaise Pascal (Pensées 277). That is to say, human thought and action are influenced in a decisive manner by what happens to the heart and in the heart. Religions, philosophies and theologies, policies and programs, whether in the church, in the state, or in international relations, are ultimately determined by a current that flows from the heart. What that potent current is and what course it takes will depend upon the heart's relationship to reality. The crucial issues in human history are related, therefore, to what happens to the heart as the dynamic center of being.

But at this point, I part company with the direction and ultimate conclusions of *Appearance and Reality*. While most grateful for the inspiration and challenge of Bradley's insights, I am committed to that Christian philosophy of life in which feeling, as life's basic dimension, has its source in a personal meeting of the human self with God, as he became manifest in Jesus Christ. The Christian Scriptures, both the Old Testament and the New, witness to an ultimate fact, which has been validated by experience through the ages: Direct contact is possible between God, the Supreme Reality, and a human being. This encounter gives birth to profound feeling, to a radical change of outlook and attitude, which results in further expressions of reality. In the upward quest of reality the Christian movement is from one reality to another, not from one appearance to another. The neo-Hegelian sequence represented by Bradley is therefore reversed.

This study will begin with reality and pass on to appearance. It will not move, as in the Oriental tradition, from the unreal to the real, nor, as in the Hellenic and Hegelian traditions, from appearance to reality. Beginning with reality, which found its supreme manifestation in a figure called Jesus and in a personal relationship to him, the God-man, it will attempt to show how in diverse facets of Christian thought and life there has been a fateful tendency through the ages to move from the real to the unreal, from Christian reality to Christian appearance, from what is authentically Christian to what looks like it but is not it.

The present volume crystallizes the author's thinking down the years on this controversial subject. The invitation to be the 1952 Currie lecturer at the midwinter convocation at the Austin Presbyterian Theological Seminary, Austin, Texas, provided the opportunity to confront systematically the issues involved. Multiple responsibilities following that memorable experience have delayed until now the publication of the Currie Lectures. In the intervening years, however, it became my privilege to deliver in substance those same lectures at the Union Theological Seminary, Buenos Aires, Argentina, and subsequently in several Asian lands where I was the Joseph Cooke Lecturer in 1960–61. In these last years, events have taken place and the situation in the church and in the world has so changed that still greater relevancy can be claimed for the perspective presented and the ideas expressed in the Austin lectures nearly two decades ago.

May I convey to Dr. David L. Stitt, the distinguished president of Austin Seminary, my profound gratitude for the privilege of being able to share my thoughts on Christian reality and appearance with students, faculty, and alumni of an institution which I have come to love and admire. And may I, at the same time, express my sincere regret that so many years should have elapsed before the publication of this book.

But perhaps God, not mere human frailty, may have played a part in this delay. Fresh developments have taken place in the realms of thought and life, in the church and in the world, to the right and to the left, that have helped to mature my thought. These developments have also provided fresh data that validate to a still greater degree the basic thesis and concern of *Christian Reality and Appearance*.

JOHN A. MACKAY

Chapter 1

CHRISTIAN REALITY

THE SHADOWS THAT BETRAY IT

The Christian religion has reached another crucial moment in its history. Across the boundaries of ecclesiastical tradition—Roman, Eastern Orthodox, and Protestant—a large proportion of those who bear the name "Christian" are characterized by religious nominalism and theological illiteracy. Their conventional association with the name of Christ neither shapes their living nor controls their thinking. To a phenomenal degree, appearance has replaced reality. At the same time, however, in the historical churches and outside them, in the secular as well as in the religious order, we witness the emergence of a fresh vitality and concern which augurs the advent of a blended renaissance and reformation. For that reason, a study of what constitutes Christian reality in its diverse facets seems particularly opportune at this time. To this study we now address ourselves.

In this introductory chapter, my endeavor will be to set in perspective, as clearly and succinctly as I can, the ground to be traversed in our thinking, the basic issues to be discussed, and the concerns that these issues engender. The remaining chapters will be devoted to a separate discussion of each one of these issues.

1. *Meeting God*

The soul of Christian reality is not a Christian philosophy or a Christian theology, even though both of these are essential for an understanding of it. The core of reality is a concrete, creative meeting between God and man. Being essentially a meeting between the Divine and the human, Christian reality is not an abstract ultimate. It is not an idea or an ideology. Its essence is not that of an instinct, an intuition, or a theory, which moves man toward a personal supernatural being or toward the ontological ground of all being, whether above him, around him, or within him. It is rather a *meeting* in which God takes the initiative and which becomes for man a transforming experience that changes his life, illumines his thought, and shapes his destiny. This encounter gives birth to a profound and abiding *feeling*.

But the question immediately arises, Does not this affirmation take the reality of God for granted? This is a very legitimate query.

We live in an era when Deity is suspect. This is true even in some Christian circles. God's existence is being challenged. If he ever did exist, is he not now "dead"? To allege that God is a concrete reality in one's daily life and relevant to the major issues with which one wrestles in contemporary affairs is to invite a smile or create disdain.

Most germane to the current mood, as symbolized by the death-of-God thesis, is a sonnet written many years ago by that Spanish poet-philosopher and prophet, Miguel de Unamuno. This poetic gem, which bears the ironic title "The Atheist's Prayer" ("La Oración del Ateo") opens thus:

> Hear my prayer, Thou God who dost not exist.
> How great Thou art, my God! Thou art so great
> That Thou art just idea.

It concludes:

> I suffer on account of Thee,
> Thou non-existent Deity. For if didst Thou really exist,
> Then would I too in truth exist.
>
> (author's translation)

The insight of this poem was never more significant than today. What could be more meaningful or more contemporaneously relevant than the intuitive recognition that true human existence is inseparably related to the existence and recognition of God?

Persons there are, of course, whose egocentricity, involving the claim and determination to be divinities in their own right, challenges this changeless reality. While being intuitively aware that the fulfillment of his own selfhood is linked to its surrender to the "Eternal Goodness," man is so constituted that his proud egotistic craving for grandeur, to be a "god" in his own right, leads him to deny God's reality. But this denial of the existence of Deity is inseparably bound to a spiritual awareness that a human cannot be really man, that he cannot "exist" in humanity's full dimension, unless he is prepared to take his intuition seriously, deny his proud self, become God's man, and thus achieve true manhood. Only when man takes seriously his own finitude and becomes related to God's infinitude does he really fulfill his own nature and assure his true destiny. For true existence means dependence upon a reality greater than one's self.

The question now arises, however, What precisely does "meeting" God signify as the core of Christian reality?

In the first place, it does not mean that he who "meets" God undergoes *absorption into Deity*. This would involve the divinization of humanity whereby man would lose his human identity. In such a case, Christian reality would be simply a phase of pantheism, and the human individual would become totally lost in the divine. Neither does Christian reality, as we interpret it, signify a contemporary expression of ancient Gnosticism in which Greek philosophy and Oriental mysticism combined to move man's mind and heart into a total identification with his environment. To be "really" Christian does not mean becoming absorbed into any specific "way" of thought or life that happens to dominate the national or world scene. Nor yet is meeting God, as portrayed in the biblical tradition, analogous in any way to the theosophical way whereby man, by the help of secret divine wisdom and through discipline, resignation, and purgation, is wheeled upward toward reality in cyclic motion. Theosophically understood, the divine-human encounter takes place in life as an endless cycle, not as an historical road.

In the second place, meeting God is not to be identified with the *possession of God*, even when the encounter is marked by passionate devotion on man's part, whereby a devoted human spirit can exclaim with meaning and sincerity, "Thou art my God." Man does not become the possessor of God, whether as an object of worship or as an instrument of manipulation. It has to be recognized, however, that among the great Spanish mystics, who were profoundly evangelical in spirit and suffered severely at the hands of their church's hierarchy, there were persons passionately devoted to God who, in the Hispanic spirit of boundless possessiveness, claimed to make God their "captive." Let me translate a verse from that great Castilian saint, Theresa of Avila. Says the mystic poetess:

> This divine union of love in which I live
> Makes God my captive, and my heart free.
> But it causes in me such pain
> To see God my prisoner
> That I die of longing to die.

(author's translation)

Theresa "met" God for the first time in her life after she had lived many years in a convent. Following that meeting, her total life and outlook became changed. She had seraphic experiences of Deity after God had become her "captive," yet no one in Christian history became more concretely and lovingly God's lowly servant than did she.

The Hispanic tradition offers still another interpretation of what a God-man meeting involves. In a famous essay entitled "My Religion," Unamuno identifies such an encounter as one of *endless struggle*. Says Don Miguel, "My religion is constant and indefatigable struggle with mystery. My religion is to struggle with God from daybreak to nightfall, as we are told Jacob struggled" (author's translation). Now, to meet God can and does involve struggle. But this encounter is more than unending struggle. It can result in inward calm, in a fresh outlook, as it actually did in the case of Jacob, not in a peace that spells death, the "peace of the sepulcher," which Unamuno decried as the tragedy of traditional religion in his country. It can give birth to the advent of a new life whose biblical symbol is the "peace like a river," about which Isaiah speaks. In the wake of meeting God in the full Christian dimension of that encounter, man is seized by a force and inspired by a vision which moves him to struggle on for the achievement of God's purpose both within him and through him. In such a case, a peace possesses his spirit which does not make him complacent or detach him from reality. It will rather be like water channeled in a river bed that swirls over rocks and surges through deep ravines on its "peaceful" way to the plains and the ocean beyond. Truly to meet God is followed by creative action. It does not end in mere ecstasies or in the evolvement of a theology.

2. *The Encounters That Shaped Reality*

Having considered what the meeting between man and God is *not*—not absorption into Deity, not the possession of Deity, not continuing struggle with Deity—the way is prepared for a presentation of the concept basic to this study, namely, that Christian reality in its essential character is a personal relationship between God and man. In this relationship, man voluntarily and joyously becomes God's servant and dedicates his whole selfhood to the fulfillment in love of God's purpose for the world.

Two events stand out, one in the Old Testament, the other in the New, which provide the historical foundation for this concept of Christian reality. They also offer the most appropriate symbols for presenting that reality. One of these events centers in the figure of a Chaldean called Abraham; the other, in the figure of a Galilean named Jesus.

At seventy-five years of age, around the year 2000 B.C., a man belonging to Ur of the Chaldees became a nomad and took up final residence in a land called Canaan. This he did because of his encounter with Ultimate Being. A spiritual reality hitherto unknown to him and his contemporaries met and spoke to Abraham. To the words of the Almighty, the man Abraham listened and responded; "Go from your country and your kindred and your father's house," said the voice, "to the land that I will show you . . . and I will bless you, and make your name great, so that you will be a blessing" (Gen. 12:1 f.). This encounter, these words, and the Chaldean's obedient response to them made world history by introducing into the religious history of man the true meaning and dimension of a divine-human relationship. God took the initiative. He met man. He called man to commitment and to action. When man obeys God, as did Abraham, he becomes God's "servant" and "friend," and a "son of Abraham."

Referring to this historic event and its significance, an English professor of philosophy, H. A. Hodges, an Anglican layman, speaks of the *"Abrahamic Presupposition."* In his book *Christianity and the Modern World View* Hodges says:

> . . . the true Christian is the spiritual child of Abraham . . . Abraham is the story of a man who has committed himself unconditionally into the hands of God; a man who does what God asks of him without hesitation, however paradoxical or

self-contradictory it may seem, and who accepts God's prom-
ises, however mysterious and incredible they may appear. It
is by virtue of this unconditional self-commitment to God that
he has won the title of the Friend of God. But such an attitude evidently presupposes a great deal. It presupposes not
merely the existence of God, about which the philosophers
have debated so lengthily, but that God is of a certain
character. . . .

The Abrahamic presupposition differs in obvious ways
from the scientific presupposition, but it has the same logical
properties and status. It is not a self-evident truth, nor a piece
of knowledge gathered from experience, but a presupposition
made as a result of a basic acceptance. It is prejustified because
it enables us to open up a field of experience which cannot be
opened up without it, and discoveries in which, if made,
would have a close bearing on human interests (pp. 28 f.).

This is a philosophical way of saying that man truly "exists,"
becomes man in the full dimension of manhood, only when
he responds completely to God and thereby becomes like
Abraham, God's man.

The New Testament event is related to Abraham's greatest son, a carpenter from Nazareth in Galilee. From the Abrahamic presupposition with its emphasis upon the necessity of
man's commitment to God, a presupposition which has abiding validity, we move to the evangelical presupposition of
God's commitment to man. This presupposition is the affirmation of an event, the most revolutionary event in terrestrial
and cosmic history. That event is this: God Almighty,
creator of the universe and Lord of history, who in an historic moment became the God of Abraham, took human
form twenty centuries later in a child named Jesus. Born in
Bethlehem, this boy reached manhood in Nazareth and engaged in a unique ministry of word and deed throughout
Palestine for a period of three years. At the close of his brief
ministry, he was crucified and three days later was resurrected
from the grave.

The incarnation of God in Jesus of Nazareth gave God, man, and history a new dimension. The poet W. H. Auden in his Christmas oratorio *For the Time Being* provides deep insight into the significance for mankind of the birth of Jesus Christ. Into the mouths of the wise men from the Orient as they gaze at "Bethlehem's Babe," Auden puts these words: "O here and now our endless journey stops." Into the mouths of the shepherds as they gaze at the infant in the manger, he puts equally significant words: "O here and now our endless journey starts."

What did the poet mean to say? Human wisdom, personified in the Magi, had reached the climactic moment in its agelong quest for ultimate meaning. At last, intellectual supermen encountered him who was the "wisdom of God" in the light of whom God and man, life and death, and the march of history were to be interpreted. In the same period simple, unsophisticated, impoverished shepherds, symbolic representatives of the human proletariat, became aware that for them life in its true dimension was now to begin. For he whom they encountered in the manger was the "power of God," one whose concern for the total welfare of common folk, coupled with the needed power to achieve it, was destined to open a new highway of hope and to insure the start of a new era of blessing.

In the incarnation of Jesus Christ, God and man not only *met* and communed, as did God and Abraham; they became *one forever*, the timeless source of light and strength. In Jesus of Nazareth is found the personalized core of Christian reality. He it is who, by the being he was, the words he spoke, the life he lived, the death he died, the new life into which he entered, the new humanity he created by the spirit he sent into the world—he will have the last word in history as the redeemer and judge of men. A man, therefore, is really Christian when he is personally related to Jesus Christ. When an individual responds to Christ's ceaseless quest by making a total commitment to the one who seeks him, he becomes aware of the truth of these poetic lines, whose author is unknown:

> I sought the Lord, and afterward I knew
> He moved my soul to seek Him seeking me;
> It was not I that found, O Saviour true;
> No, I was found of Thee.

Here is something to be stressed and never forgotten. The meeting, the personal relationship between God and man, which constitutes the very essence of Christian reality, is not the mere climax of man's spiritual quest for God. It is the culmination of God's quest for man, a quest which became historically and symbolically manifest in the figures of Abraham and Jesus Christ.

3. *The Christian Quadrilateral*

Let me at this point concentrate our gaze on one of the great New Testament images which gives poetic and theological significance to the proposition native to this study— that Christian reality, whose foundation is a God-man relationship, is composed of four distinctive facets. I refer to the apocalyptic vision of "a new heaven and a new earth" and of "the holy city, new Jerusalem, coming down out of heaven from God, prepared as a bride adorned for her husband" (Rev. 21:1 f.). Simultaneously, a "great voice from the throne" was heard saying, "Behold, the dwelling of God is with men" (v. 3), to be followed by a proclamation by the same voice, "Behold, I make all things new" (v. 5).

This particular image did not originate, but it did inspire, the present interpretation of Christian reality as having four constituent and inseparable elements. The emergence in history of the new reality, the "holy city," which is associated with total renovation, presents a symbolic structure that has profound significance. In this new structure, this city, with its foursquare wall (v. 16) whose foundations are the "twelve apostles of the Lamb" (v. 14), there is no temple, no established center of religious activity. The center of the city's light and life is "the Lord God the Almighty and the Lamb" (v. 22). The Lamb is the city's lamp, in which is concentrated as its center of diffusion and luminous medium, the full splendor of Deity. Striking and significant is the fact that into this city, with its ever-open gates and ever-shining light, shall come the "kings of the earth" with all the majesty of the secular order (vss. 22–27). This vision of the Seer of Patmos regarding the Christ-centered consummation that would mark history's close provided a major source for Handel's Hallelujah Chorus, "He [Christ] shall reign for ever and ever."

From this apocalyptic vision, with its mystic and poetic beauty and profound theological significance, I have drawn lifelong inspiration. But so far as concerns the present study, my indebtedness is limited to the Seer's description of the city wall as being "four-square." My adoption of the quadrilateral dimension of this symbolic reality of the four walls that surrounded the holy city is not to be considered the fruit of revelation! It is rather the literary adaptation of a biblical symbol to express thoughts and convictions which are the fruit of my reflection that Christian reality has four distinctive but inseparably related facets. To the exploration of this quadrilateral dimension, let us now address ourselves.

Each of the four constitutive elements of Christian reality, if true to its own essential nature, is distinguishable from, but inseparably related to, the other three. It is equally true, and it is an ironic and tragic fact, that each one of the four facets that together constitute Christian reality is reproduced by something that looks like it but is not it. But this something, while being no more than appearance—reality's shadow—

can become an idolatrous substitute for reality. Following a brief preliminary presentation of what constitutes Christian reality and appearance, I will pass on to a more basic and extensive exploration of each facet of the real and of what in each instance is merely appearance, a substitutionary shadow.

Here are the constitutive facets of Christian reality:

1. God's Self-Disclosure.
2. The Transforming Encounter.
3. The Community of Christ.
4. Christian Obedience.

The betraying shadows of Christian reality, I designate thus:

1. Theologism: The Idolatry of Ideas.
2. Impressionism: The Idolatry of Feeling.
3. Churchism: The Idolatry of Structure.
4. Ethicism: The Idolatry of Prescripts.

Let me now offer a brief interpretative survey of this religious paradox and then proceed to a fuller study of the facets of the Christian quadrilateral.

4. The Essential Facets of Christian Reality

A. *God's Self-Disclosure.* The Bible is acknowledged to be literature's greatest masterpiece. It is also the supreme source of the Christian's knowledge of God and God's activity. It deals essentially with God's revelation of himself and his purpose for mankind. God disclosed himself progressively to persons descended from an individual called Abraham. Those persons appeared in different epochs of Abrahamic history as lawgivers, monarchs, prophets, and poets. Finally and supremely, God made himself manifest in human history by becoming incarnate in Jesus Christ, Abraham's greatest son. This son of Abraham and of God became the Savior and

Lord of life. He founded a community called the church, which today is found on all the frontiers of the world. Jesus Christ spoke to man about God, lived for man in the love of God, died for man upon a cross, rose again from the dead, sent forth into the world the Holy Spirit, who "proceedeth from the Father and the Son." The Spirit's chief role in history is to give vitality to the proclamation of the gospel by those commissioned by Christ, the "Good News" of what God has done and is doing in Christ, and also to "guide . . . into all truth" (John 16:13) those who become Christ's disciples. While "seated at the right hand of God" (Col. 3:1), Jesus Christ is also found on the road of life, in the heart and at the side of all who "accept him as their Savior and serve him as their king in the fellowship of his church."

It is one of the timeless Christian imperatives that all who take God's self-disclosure seriously shall cultivate an intelligent understanding of their faith. They must love God with the mind. In loyalty to God's self-disclosure as set forth in Holy Scripture, in concern about the upbuilding and stability of the church, and as a contribution to human thought, Christians, under the guidance of the Holy Spirit and with due sensitivity to the life and problems of men, must create and maintain a Christian theology.

Christian doctrines and creeds are essential media whereby an intellectual dimension is given to Christian reality. They constitute instruments by means of which visibility is given to the spiritually real; they also provide an intellectual foundation for Christian thought and life. Doctrines are like telescopic and microscopic lenses that make visible and facilitate the interpretation of objects and relationships, which otherwise would not be discernible nor seen in appropriate perspective.

B. *The Transforming Encounter.* God's self-disclosure of himself, which constitutes the objective, historical dimension of Christian reality, gave birth and continues to give birth to a subjective dimension—the dimension of personal religious experience. What God did *for* man in Christ is followed by what he does *in* man through Christ. He meets man; he communes with man; he changes man. When man takes God seriously, responding in love to God's love for him, he becomes a new man, "God's man." From thinking about God and longing for God, he experiences God. The God whom he has encountered and who has changed the direction of his life, becomes for the "new man" both a living presence and a compulsive power.

This dimension of Christian experience, involving the awareness of a personal relationship to God, bears witness to the fact that God individualizes. It gives concrete expression to the objective reality of grace, God's movement toward man, and to subjective reality of faith, the biblical term for man's responsive movement toward God. It also gives abiding status, meaning, and spiritual contemporaneity to the book of Psalms, in which we listen to moving conversation between God and man. Says the God of the Universe to a simple person in a rustic community, "I have called you by your name. You are mine." Says a confiding, anonymous individual to Deity, "You are *my* God."

This divine-human encounter takes many forms. The degree of consciousness on the part of the individual who experiences it may vary greatly. The meeting may take place quietly or dramatically. The person involved may not even be aware of the place or the time of its first occurrence. But what matters is the reality of the event, and the continuing sense of the presence. Important also, of course, is the evidence of the person's likeness in daily living to him who is the "truth and the life." What matters is not *how* or *when* one had an experience of God that made "all things new." The important thing is the *fact* of rebirth, and the tangible proof, subjective and objective, that one's life is God-centered and is oriented toward God's Kingdom of truth and righteousness. At the core of the new life is the love of God and of others. In the words of Jonathan Edwards, *"True religion, in great part, consists in holy affections"* (*Treatise Concerning the Religious Affections*). These holy affections find expression in the worship of God, in the service of God, and in fellowship with like-minded people as members together of the church of Christ.

C. *The Community of Christ.* The communal dimension of Christian reality witnesses to the fact that while to be really Christian a person must have a direct relationship to God, there is at the same time no place for pure individualism. The "new men in Christ" are members of a fellowship, a community of faith called the church, a unique association created by Christ through the Holy Spirit. This historic community was born in dramatic form at Pentecost. From its inception the church gave expression to its universal character, across all linguistic boundaries. It expressed also the reality and practical implications of loving God and one another. It was hailed by the apostles and early Christians as the "New Israel," the "Israel of God," the "fellowship of the Spirit." Where was the church to be found? How could it be identified? In the course of the years a dictum became current, "Where Christ is, there is the church." In the contemporary era, the German-Swiss theologian Karl Barth has given expression to the Apostolic and post-Apostolic interpretation of the church as community by saying that the church is the fellowship of all those for whom Jesus Christ is Lord, the living congregation of the living Lord Jesus Christ.

While community is the core of churchly reality, the community must, for both religious and secular reasons, become organized. It must create for itself a visible organizational structure. In the course of the centuries, the Christian church has had, and continues to have, many diverse structural forms. But amid all the changes through which the church passes and whatever its organizational shape may be, across all boundaries of culture and race, of ocean, mountain and forest, there are certain changeless centralities that must be observed by all members of the community of Christ.

First, the finality of the church is changeless. It exists to bear witness to Christ and the gospel in its way of life, its forms of thought, and its course of action, taking seriously Christ's mandate to make him known to all men, to the uttermost bounds of human habitation. By so doing, the community of Christ will, in the love of God, in the love of men, and in the love of one another, give worldwide reality to a totally new type and dimension of human community.

Second, the form of organizational structure adopted by a Christian community, wherever it is located throughout the world, must be guided by this principle. Under the direction of the Holy Spirit and in loyalty to the nature and requirements of the Christian community as set forth in Holy Scripture, church organization must be such as to enable the church to "be the church," in the particular environment in which its members live and witness. That is to say, the church must not seek to absolutize a given organizational structure to such a degree that the structure becomes, in a subtle manner and with disastrous consequences, an end in itself and in this way a substitute for what the church exists to be. The church is truly the church and can fulfill its function within its environment and in history only when it accepts itself as an *instrument*, a medium which God uses to "prepare the way of the Lord," that the Kingdom of God may come. The church's life and witness must be for the sake of the Kingdom. Under the lordship of Christ, the church must operate as a redemptive, reconciling reality in every facet of human life and relationships. To use the luminous words of John Calvin, the church is in essence, and must be willing to be in its existence, "the instrument of God's glory." In the life and thought of its members, individually and corporately, it must give visible expression to the character of God and his reconciling purpose for mankind.

In order that the church may be able to achieve its supreme finality and express its truly instrumental character as a community of destiny in this world and in the world to come, all its members must take their identity seriously as belonging to the body of Christ. They must therefore be educated and prepared for the fulfillment of their role as followers of Christ and members of the "household of God." For that reason, the church today must be awakened to give contemporary meaning to the injunction of the Apostle Paul in his letter to the Ephesians that the "saints," "God's men and women," in a word, Christians, be "properly equipped for their service" (4:12, Phillips' translation). According to Paul the clergy, that is, the full-time professional leaders of the church, have it as their role to prepare the laity "for the work of ministry" (Eph. 4:12). It is the responsibility of each Christian to be a minister, that is, "a servant." And it is the responsibility of the church organization to see to it that each member becomes just that. Only so, can the church and its members take their calling seriously.

D. *Christian Obedience.* Obedience, action, truth that inspires goodness, fellowship that is fulfilled in service, community that takes to the road—all are constituent elements of what it means to belong to the church, which is Christ's body. "You are my friends," said Jesus on one occasion to his followers, "if you do what I command you" (John 15:14). While belonging to a fellowship, Christians cannot be just "buddies" of the fellowship director or of one another. The goal of Christian fellowship is not merely to have a good time together, however inspiring that may be. The members of the fellowship must act, sometimes corporately, sometimes individually, often in tragic loneliness as they confront a difficult and complex issue. But they must always take action as committed Christians for whom obedience to Christ is the supreme imperative, the life of Christ the inspiring pattern, a sense of the presence of Christ the chief consolation, and a conscience sensitized by Christ the ultimate norm for decision and action.

While there are principles and objectives that should guide Christian behavior, while Christians have the assurance of light and strength for daily living, situations arise, crossroads are reached, that confront them with dilemmas. This is so even when they take seriously both biblical truth and him who is the truth, and also, the advice of fellow Christians. It is then that the cross and the crucified take on a new dimension. It is then that Christians, as individuals or as groups, have to tread the road of suffering in loyalty to truth as they understand it, in relation to the situation as they see it, and in accordance with their conscience as they feel it. We have today reached a moment in history when crisis in the church and in society is so acute and confusion so widespread regarding law and order that the question of Christian ethics and of what it means to be truly "Christian" in action awakens growing concern and demands increasing attention. That is to say, the ethical dimension of Christian reality needs fresh exploration in the context of the present situation in the church and in the world.

5. *The Betrayers*

Shadows at this point appear on the horizon of Christian reality. Let us glance briefly at some idolatrous substitutes for the Real. In the following chapters I will attempt an analytical and detailed description of these substitutes. It is important, however, that, before we engage in a fuller study, the reader be aware of what constitutes each of these phenomena.

A. The first idolatrous substitute for Christian reality I call *theologism: the idolatry of ideas*. By that I mean the practice of transforming ideas into realities. Loyalty to ideas *about* the Bible, *about* God, *about* Jesus Christ, and *about* other Christian realities becomes a substitute for loyalty to God, to the Bible, to Jesus Christ, and also for authentic Christian behavior. Let us be quite clear at this point: Theological concepts are important and necessary to depict reality and to clarify its nature, but they do not constitute the reality itself. A man can say, "I believe the Bible from cover to cover," without taking seriously what the Bible says. One can give allegiance to the most orthodox concepts about Jesus Christ without giving allegiance to Jesus Christ himself. Christian doctrines, creeds, confessions, are indispensable. But they are instruments, media, whereby Christian reality is intellectually discerned and a theological basis is provided for the illumination and institutional unification of the Christian community. Whenever ideas, of whatever kind, are given the status of being the ultimate object of Christian devotion, they become idols and their devotees become idolaters.

B. The same can happen in the realm of feeling, giving rise to *impressionism: the idolatry of emotion.* To meet God, to have a continuing awareness of God's reality, is inseparably related to feeling, to the heart. Christian emotion receives expression in a great variety of ways. The precise form of expression depends upon the experience and temperament of the persons involved, the particular tradition to which they belong, and the cultural situation in which they live. Hence, the vast diversity in the literature of devotion, the styles of church architecture, the forms of both private and public worship, the types of witness given to a personal experience of God. But whenever an emotional thrill is sought for its own sake, becoming in itself the substance of Christian experience or worship, we move from reality to appearance, from God to idols. It is a tragic fact that the emotional thrill derived from sights and sounds that are the aesthetic accompaniments of the public worship of God can become, and in a multitude of instances do become, substitutes for genuine encounter with God.

It is possible for a person to spend long hours in a shrine of architectural beauty and grandeur, to participate in a religious service of liturgical splendor, to be more emotionally moved than when seated in the theater witnessing a classical drama; and yet when the service ends and he crosses the threshold of the sanctuary homeward bound, he may retain no more than the memory of an aesthetic thrill. He returns in loneliness to life's routine, without the experience of a presence with whom he enjoyed contact and from whom he received fresh light and strength for daily living.

Let this not be forgotten, however. While it is possible to substitute the idol of religious feeling for devotion to God, another idol no less subtle can take God's place in the subjective realm. At the opposite extreme from liturgical addicts, there are people extremely conservative who so magnify the emotion experienced by a direct encounter with God that their witness to God consists in endless narration of the details of that encounter. To recount the emotional accompaniments of their original meeting with God becomes an idolatrous substitute for witness to the abiding reality of God's presence on the road of life. For that reason, they never grow up. They remain devotees of a cult of emotion.

C. A similar phenomenon afflicts the church, which I call *churchism: the idolatry of structure.* The Christian church, as we have observed and stressed, was born as a community of people personally committed to Jesus Christ. But naturally, like every community, the church became organized, and in order to function, assumed institutional form. As time went on, it appeared under the guise of many structures. While communal reality did not disappear, its importance in many instances diminished. At the same time, increasing significance was attached to the organization, and increasing power was vested in its leadership. The moment came when the church's leaders proclaimed that they constituted the church. They ceased to be the church's servants and became its lords. In the meantime, the church itself ceased to be God's servant and became his patron, assuming the role and rights of Deity. For many members it became more important to belong to the church and to obey it than to belong to God and to obey him. The church institution thus became the visible, historical expression of Christian reality and the supreme object of Christian allegiance. Reality gave place to appearance. An organization created to serve became an idol to be adored.

While this trend became most ominous in the great hierarchical churches, especially the Roman, its presence was not lacking in the church denominations of Protestantism. Following the Reformation, sectarian groups emerged who considered themselves to be the church and assumed a spirit of arrogance and complacency. Promethean institutional pride has afflicted the community of Christ through the ages and has confronted the Head of the community with many problems, both tragic and ironic. False doctrinal assumptions and sinful personal pretensions have produced ecclesiastical idols. For that reason, the problem of the church's renewal has a dimension much greater than is currently recognized by those concerned Christians who have made a slogan of the apocalyptic words, "Behold, I make all things new."

At the present juncture in Christian history, when the ancient term "ecumenical" has been rediscovered and is being given widely divergent connotations, there has emerged in certain sectors of Protestantism the idea that the church can "be the church," and the meaning of "ecumenical" unity can be truly expressed, only when the church has achieved institutional oneness. This new manifestation of churchism, the current aberration that afflicts the ecumenical movement, will be given due consideration at a later point in this study.

D. We come finally to what I call *ethicism*. By ethicism, I mean the form of obedience to codes, mandates, injunctions, that is equated with obedience to God and is considered the practical expression of Christian reality in its moral dimension. In many instances loyalty to law and to an existing form of social or political order is given precedence over loyalty to Christ, to the Kingdom of God, and to a just society.

One of the most basic issues in Christian history, past and present, relates to the status of action in Christian living. What is the kind of action in which Christians should engage, and what is the source from which they should derive their inspiration for acting in a particular instance? At this point, and in anticipation of what will be dealt with in the final chapter, this alone needs to be said: In the realm of morals, two extremes must be rejected. One extreme is the idolatry of law. By this, I mean the isolation and absolutization of any one commandment of the Decalogue, without setting it in the perspective of the other nine, and of the imperatives inspired by the gospel and by the Kingdom of God. This legalistic extremism can also involve Christians as citizens in adherence to an absolute imperative imposed by a secular government, a mandate that may run counter to the will of God and to their Christian consciences.

The other extreme, equally to be avoided, is this: There are occasions when a human situation is so tragic and arouses such deep concern that a Christian is tempted to justify and even to deify whatever form of action is adopted to bring that situation to an end. There is, for example, the question of the use of violence.

We are now ready to move onward to examine more fully the several facets of Christian reality and their idolatrous counterparts.

Chapter II

GOD'S SELF-DISCLOSURE
&
THE IDOLATRY OF IDEAS

Amid the changes in our changing world, there is a changeless truth. The eternal God has made himself known to mankind. He has spoken to wayward, self-centered man and become redemptively involved in human history. God's revelation of himself to an aged Chaldean called Abraham and in a young Galilean called Jesus, together with the implications for human thought and life involved in this dual disclosure, constitutes the first facet of Christian reality. It is important to have a clear understanding of the redemptive coming of God into the life of man as recorded in the Bible, and at the same time, what can happen when ideas regarding the reality of God's concerned presence in history become substitutes for the reality itself.

1. *History's Supreme Event*

Having dealt extensively in the last chapter with the question of God's being, let us now concentrate attention upon his self-disclosure. God disclosed his identity, presence, and purpose in the life history of a people descended from Abraham, who had responded adventurously to a voice from the unknown. He disclosed his substance in a person called Jesus, a being truly God and truly man, who was crucified. God disclosed his power in the resurrection of Jesus Christ from the dead. He unfolded his purpose in the manifestation and abiding presence of his Spirit, by whom was brought into being a new community called the church, the "New Israel." This communal reality was designed to be the organ for the fulfillment of God's redemptive purpose in Christ. The authoritative record and interpretation of God's progressive self-disclosure is contained in the Scriptures of the Old and New Testaments, which are a literary legacy of the Holy Spirit given to mankind through the church.

The focal center of God's self-disclosure is Jesus Christ. He is the personal manifestation of the presence and action of Almighty God. The centrality of Christ in the Christian faith is dramatically and luminously set forth in the final discourse of Christianity's first martyr, a man called Stephen, whose death was witnessed and applauded by a Jewish fanatic from Tarsus named Saul.

In the historical perspective of the appearance of the "God of glory" to "our father Abraham" (Acts 7:2) and of God's direct impact upon the lives of Abraham and his influential descendants, Joseph, Moses, Joshua, David and Solomon, Stephen upbraided the leaders of Judaism for their total insensitivity to what the "Most High" was doing in their time. He charged that, in line with the traditional hostility of their forbears to the demand of prophetic figures to take seriously God's claim upon the total life of man, they betrayed and murdered the "Righteous One," Jesus Christ (Acts 7:52). Moments later, as Stephen was being stoned to death, he uttered words that enshrine his conviction, hope, and spirit. With uplifted eyes, and an awareness that the crucified was now the triumphant Lord, "at the right hand of God," he addressed to him these words: "Lord Jesus, receive my spirit" (v. 59). And then, inspired by the spirit and example of the Man of Calvary, he prayed for his murderers thus: "Lord, do not hold this sin against them" (v. 60).

It was not long thereafter that Saul the Tarsan, described in this narrative as "consenting to Stephen's death," had an encounter with Stephen's Lord. While on a hate mission to Damascus in quest of other disciples of the Galilean, who should suffer Stephen's fate, a light suddenly flashed across his path and a voice sounded, "Saul, Saul, why do you persecute me?" (Acts 9:4). The brutal hate-mongering zealot was converted. Not long thereafter, he himself was being persecuted for his devotion to him who met him on the road and who became the motive of his thought, the heart of his heart, and the lifelong companion of his missionary career.

The Christ-centeredness of Paul's thought, life, and mission has profound significance for Christian theology today. The person who can legitimately be described as Christianity's greatest apostle, greatest thinker, greatest mystic, greatest saint, found in Jesus Christ his deepest understanding and experience of the reality of God and of what it means to be a real man and to live a truly human life.

Very moving and relevant at this point in our study are the stanzas of a poem *Saint Paul*, written by an English poet-scholar, Frederic W. H. Myers. The first stanza reads:

CHRIST! I am Christ's! and let the name suffice you,
  Ay, for me too He greatly hath sufficed:
Lo, with no winning words I would entice you,
  Paul has no honour and no friend but Christ.

The last stanza runs thus:

Yea thro' life, death, thro' sorrow and thro' sinning
  He shall suffice me, for he hath sufficed:
Christ is the end, for Christ was the beginning,
  Christ the beginning, for the end is Christ.

As has been repeatedly emphasized in this study, the self-disclosure of God is inseparably related to the Bible. The Bible sets forth the epic of God's quest for man which began with Abraham, which culminated in Christ, and which created a new type of human community called the church. This epic, and all that is involved in it and that is said about

it in the Bible, is God's word to man. In the Bible, as no-
where else, we are able to see in its full dimension the life of
man in the light of God and to discover the clue to an understanding of the human problem and the key to its solution.
But, to understand the "strange new world" described in the
book, one must have "eyes of faith." To become part of this
new world, a person must commit himself in the spirit of
Stephen and Paul and their evangelical successors to Christ
crucified and risen, who is in a supreme sense the Word of
God incarnate and about whom the Bible speaks and to whom
it points. Let me repeat: The Bible is a book about Jesus
Christ, who is the "light of the world" and in whose light we
see light. To refer once again to that famous passage in the
book of Revelation, Christ is the lamp in which is concentrated the total light of Deity.

2. *Theology, the Adjunct of Reality*

We are now ready to move forward to what I call the
inseparable adjunct of Christian reality, by which I mean
theology. The full dimension of Christian reality as God's
self-disclosure cannot be apprehended in a way worthy of
this event of such historical and cosmic significance without
the use of ideas and the formulation of doctrine. Theology
is an indispensable instrument for understanding and presenting what God has done, has said, and proposes to accom-
plish. Justice cannot be done to God's quest for man, to man's
response to God, nor to the implications of both, without the
responsible creation of creeds, confessions, and theological
systems. Moreover, because of the current confusion in Christian circles, a theology that is true to the changeless and sensitive to the changing is a major imperative as never before in
history. But such a theology, and indeed all theology, must
be instrumental in character. Doctrine must not claim to be

itself reality, but to be a true and necessary instrument by means of which reality is discerned, defined, and embraced. In a word, Christian theology, while not being itself a constitutive part of Christian reality, is its inseparable adjunct.

So understood, a theological system is like a telescope or a microscope. The telescope does not itself create reality, but it clarifies what is visible to the eyes though distant from them and enables the mind to form a judgment as to the significance of what is discerned. The microscope equips the eye to see what otherwise would remain invisible and provides the mind with the data necessary for the interpretation of what is brought to light. Individual dogmas in a theological system correspond to the lenses in both telescope and microscope. These lenses need to be cleaned from time to time. They must sometimes be reground, or even replaced, to give the instrument greater potency. There are occasions, also, when the position of the lenses must be readjusted and when even the telescope as a whole must be reshaped so that the instrument may have greater power to make the object being gazed at more discernible to the eye, and its constituent elements more intelligible to the mind. While instruments like these are to be used continuously and should be accorded all honor, while they should also be made available for the admiring gaze of spectators who have become entranced by their achievements in opening up new worlds of physical reality, one thing must be avoided. These servants of science must never become mere museum pieces to be studied and admired and even idolized. Their instrumental servant-role must never cease. So must it be too with Christian creeds and confessions.

Woe to the worldwide Christian community when ideas about God take the place of God himself, when allegiance to ideas about him takes the place of allegiance to him! Whenever and wherever this happens, a new form of idolatry emerges in the Christian tradition. Tragedies that occurred in

Israel's history are reproduced in contemporary terms. The time came when the stone-engraven tablets of the Law, the wooden Ark of the Covenant, and such resounding words as "the temple of the Lord, the temple of the Lord, the temple of the Lord," with which a dissolute people repudiated Jeremiah's concern about their spiritual estate (Jer. 7:4) became idolatrous substitutes for obedience to God, for God's Covenant with Israel, and for God's real presence when truly worshipped. This phenomenon of transition from the status of instrumental medium to that of object of idolatrous adoration and symbol of assured well-being is dramatically described by the prophet Habakkuk. He describes the conversion of a fishing net into an idol: Israel "sacrifices to his net and burns incense to his seine" (Hab. 1:16).

But before I deal concretely and in contemporary terms with the tragic transition from the reality of divine revelation to its idolatrous substitution by ideas designed to describe it, let me set in perspective the importance and also the limitations of theological ideas.

3. *The Contemporary Need of Theology*

Never in Christian history was there greater need for theological thought than there is today. Some decades ago, in a period of intellectual lethargy, when theology was either ignored or disdained in important church circles, a group of concerned churchmen in the eastern United States began to advocate the "restoration of theology." They set up for clergy and laity a summer "Institute of Theology." They later established a quarterly journal *Theology Today* which circulates in more than eighty countries, to which they gave the symbolic motto, "The Life of Man in the Light of God." This effort helped awaken a new interest in theology in the United States and in other parts of the world.

The necessity for theological ideas and discussion is great and urgent. In the majority of Christian churches, the laity suffer from grave illiteracy as regards an intelligent understanding of the Christian faith. They lack sensitivity to the implications of the faith for personal relationships in the church, in the home, and in business. This is particularly tragic at a time when we witness a revolt of youth against the existing order. This revolt is marked by a sense of alienation and estrangement from the older generation, by the manifestation of anxieties and a quest for meaning, by a craving for the emergence of an impressive personality, a dynamic idea, a crusading cause as the object of their devotion. To a group of Spanish youth gripped by this mood, Miguel de Unamuno once said, "Get a great idea; marry it, found a home with it, and raise a family."

When this mood is dominant among youth, when the life of the Christian rank and file is marked by ignorance and complacency, when the problems of poverty, hunger, and racial injustice give meaning to the concept of revolutionary change, then the strains of the Communist International become alluring: "Arise ye prisoners of starvation. Arise ye wretched of the earth. For Justice thunders condemnation. A better world's in birth." At such a time, the basic theological ideas that illumine the core of Christian reality have overwhelming validity and relevancy, and need to be understood and taken seriously by all, in every sphere of life, who bear the Christian name.

Two theological ideas closely related to each other need to be reemphasized and applied today. They are the ideas of *meeting* and *caring*. The proposition that meeting, personal encounter between God and man and also between man and man, is essential for establishing a meaningful and creative relationship between the parties concerned is foundational both for true religion and for a true society. There can be no substitute for meeting, whether between estranged individuals and groups or between nations alienated from one another. And meeting involves, of course, conversation.

The second idea concerns caring. The proposition of caring, which means loving concern for people in the full dimension of their being, whether that concern be manifested by God or by man, defines the core of the Christian religion. Let me be more specific. In Christian thought and life, and in human relations in general, there can be no substitute for concerned encounter between the older and younger generations, between parents and children, between pastor and people, between teachers and students, between the rich and the poor, between government officials and common citizens, between members of all races, religions and ideologies, and even between enemies. "Christianity taught us to care. Caring matters most" (*Letters from Baron Friedrich Von Hügel to a Niece*). And caring, if it is to be more than mere condescension, is inseparably related to meeting, to the kind of meeting that was historically born in an encounter between God and a Chaldean nomad called Abraham and was theologically defined as the "Abrahamic presupposition" by another Christian layman.

Thus understood, meeting and caring received and continue to have their supreme expression in the Christian gospel. The essence of the gospel, the "good news," is this: God's "caring" for man was such that he had a unique "meeting" with him, becoming incarnate in a person, Jesus of Nazareth. It is through the life and teaching, the death and resurrection, the saviorhood and lordship of Jesus Christ the God-man that God the Almighty, the All-wise, and the All-loving made manifest, and continues to make manifest, the meaning of "caring" for man and of "meeting" him in a decisive encounter. This encounter brought into being a new humanity, the Christian church. Being itself a creation of the gospel and the corporate manifestation of God's "meeting" man and "caring" for him in Christ, the church, if it is to be true to its nature, must be an evangelical community. It must give top priority in its thinking to understanding the gospel; it must give top priority in its being to proclaiming and living the gospel. Girded with truth as a belt (Eph. 6:14), and not merely as an ideological treasure, gripped by him who is himself the truth, the church as the community of Christ must, in response to Christ's "Follow me," continue to exist as the world's chief pilgrim and crusader on the evangelical road.

4. *When Ideas Supplant Reality*

We are now ready to move another step forward. While it is true that theological ideas are important and constitute an inseparable adjunct to Christian reality, they are not themselves a constituent part of that reality. In a subtle and disastrous manner, they can become idols that supplant reality. When this happens, idea worshipers are converted into spiritual dwarfs and intellectual fanatics.

Ponder this parable. In one of his essays, "Las Hurdes," in the volume *Andanzas y Visiones Españolas,* Unamuno describes the Hurds, a primitive people living far from civilization in the mountain ravines of old Castile. The great majority of this hill tribe had their huts in a deep canyon where the sun shone for only a few hours a day. Physically they were dwarfs and suffered from cretinism, a condition of physical and mental stunting due to severe thyroid deficiency. Some of Unamuno's companions considered that this abnormality was due to the lack of sunshine, others to water pollution. But in Unamuno's judgment the real reason for the dwarfish, ailing physique of the Hurds was the fact that the water they drank was too pure. It was virtually distilled. It came straight down from the snowy peaks and was lacking in salts, especially iodine, which is so essential for the growth of the body. Unamuno carries the analogy into the realm of the spirit with this profound comment, "Those who drink only pure ideas end up suffering from spiritual cretinism. The soul that lives on categories remains a dwarf" (author's translation).

It is important that we look at the spiritual sickness and dwarfishness that results when life is lived on ideas and categories which, being extolled as pure and perfect, are given the status of divinities to be worshiped.

History abounds with examples of this ailing dwarfness. The Athenian philosophers who escorted Paul to the Areopagus in order to listen to his ideas were dwarfs in the Hellenistic tradition. Socrates, Plato, and Aristotle were committed to specific great ideas that opened up for them the way to reality, signaling the path which they themselves took. But their successors "spent their time in nothing except telling or hearing something new" (Acts 17:21). They were not interested in "marrying a great idea" but in dating ideological dames that stirred their curiosity. Reality for them was commitment to the passing show of novelty and diversity.

Those Athenians have a host of successors in the universities and theological centers of today, especially in the United States. Our centers of higher learning have become dedicated to the academic ideal of creating communities of scholars—encyclopedias and textbooks incarnate. A majority of those whose scholarship is in the liberal arts glory in being cognizant of all that has ever been thought regarding ultimate reality and the meaning of life. But such is their sense of superiority as scholars that they refuse to commit themselves to any one idea in particular. They are devotees of the cult of the uncommitted. There are signals, however, on the contemporary horizon that challenge this type of academic isolation from reality. Youth, gripped by a new mood of concern for their own future and the world's, and in quest of a dynamic philosophy of life in this revolutionary time, demand to know their teachers' convictions on basic issues. To be presented with a panorama of traditional or possible viewpoints no longer satisfies them. They say to a mentor, "But sir, we want to know what *you* think." It becomes increasingly clear that, surrounded on all sides by revolutionary change involving social justice and human rights, a university can no longer live a life of balconized detachment from the world. It must be sensitive to human reality in its immediate environment and beyond. It must not continue to equate reality with savants' ideas and books. Its leaders must be the incarnation of a learning that *cares* for people. They must not be people who have become incarnate in learning.

5. *Theological Egotism*

Theological institutions too are confronted with a crisis no less grave and challenging. The ultimates that tend to shape policy in many of these academic centers are not the changeless realities relating to God and man, however differently these realities may be expressed. The current mood of theological education tends to be the absolutization of the relative and the changing, in all their diverse facets, historical, sociological, psychological, hermeneutical, ecclesiological, procedural. This mood affects, of course, the entire theological outlook. It has special bearing upon the answers to such crucial questions as What does it mean to be a Christian, a Christian minister, a servant of the Christian community, or a citizen in today's world? and What constitutes Christian theology and what is it for?

In present-day Protestantism there is an incipient movement toward rejecting belief in the abiding structure of Christian reality. And yet, the thrilling contemporary task of Christian theology is the understanding of this reality in our revolutionary epoch and an intelligent interpretation of the timeless principles enshrined in it. For that reason, the current engrossment—the ailing obsession with the fact of change, without the changing being set in the perspective of the changeless—is part of the religious tragedy today. Instead of Christian reality being pondered to provide a clue for creative confrontation of change and instead of the life of man being studied in the light of God, the life of God, so far as his existence is admitted, is studied in the light of man. Changing man and a changing world, manifestations and schools of theological change, become the chief object of study and concern. But, after the full dimension of change in thought and life has been contemplated, the inevitable question arises, Where do we go from here? The answer is not easy. A creative answer, moreover, can never be given to this question without a changeless fact being recognized. That fact is this: Theological sophistication as an ideal of seminary education can never be a creative substitute for an understanding of Christian reality. The moment it is given this substitutionary status, it becomes appearance.

The substitution of ideas for reality takes on a quite different dimension when we consider the status of theology in churches that call themselves "orthodox." To be "orthodox" is to have "right opinions," "sound doctrines." "Orthodoxy" is a designation that has been equally adopted by church bodies in both the Eastern and Western traditions of the Christian religion. Such churches insist that they possess the truth.

I recall experiences in ecumenical gatherings in Oxford, England, several decades ago, which provide illustrations of what "orthodoxy" involves in the churches of the Oriental tradition. At one of the sessions of the Commission on the Universal Church and the World of Nations, which met in Oxford in 1937, several of the members urged that the church should express its penitence for sinful attitudes that had marked its life. In the course of the discussion, an archbishop of the Greek Orthodox Church, a most gracious and beloved personality, handed me, as chairman of the meeting, a note which said, "The Church can *not* sin."

Twelve years later, at an Oxford meeting of the "Faith and Order Commission" of the World Council of Churches, a debate took place on what constitutes Christian truth. A distinguished theologian of the Greek Orthodox Church, and a warm personal friend, remarked as the discussion continued that the question concerning truth was not an issue for his church. "Why?" I asked. "Because *we have* the truth," he answered. The Eastern Orthodox churches, as is well known, have not been missionary minded. The Great Commission has not been taken seriously. So, I quietly raised the question whether Jesus' last command to his disciples that they "make disciples of all nations" (Matt. 28:16–20) should be regarded as a part of the Christian truth. "Of course," was the reply. Whereupon I observed, "How can Christians say they *have* the truth if they do not *do* the truth?" The point was embarrassing, and the debate ended. But the issue remains. Christian truth is not something *we have*. It is something that *must have us*. It is not enough for a Christian to say he possesses the truth. He must be possesed by the truth—by that One who is himself the truth, Jesus Christ our Lord. True ideas are not themselves reality. Their ultimate role is to lead us to reality. Orthodoxy, whatever its name or claims, must be validated by the life and action of those who exult in possessing this ideational badge.

At the opposite ecclesiastical pole from Greek and Russian Orthodoxy are Protestants who glory in being "orthodox." They revel in the theological purity of their ideas, but they are nevertheless in very many instances spiritual dwarfs. They frequently betray the gospel by unethical behavior and bring evangelical Christianity into disrepute. Let me be more specific. Persons there are who glory in their loyalty to the Bible: "I believe in the Bible from cover to cover," you hear one exclaim. "No one can accuse me of being a heretic." Yet he himself does not take the Bible seriously. He does not listen to the book. He does not attend to the voice that speaks through it. He substitutes ideas about words and the status of words for a confrontation with him who is himself the Word, the core of the biblical message and the clue to the Bible's meaning. When this happens, the Bible ceases to be a means of salvation, the supreme medium of God's encounter with man and the vehicle of his grace. It becomes simply an object of worship, an idol. Tragedy ensues. There are Bible worshippers whose spiritual lives are literally pagan.

So, too, as regards Jesus Christ, there are those who have the most orthodox ideas about Christ. But, while being committed to the truth of his incarnation, his virgin birth, his God-manhood, his vicarious death, his resurrection from the dead, his ascension to God's right hand, and his coming again in glory, their ultimate loyalty is given to ideas concerning Christ, not to Christ himself as a living reality. They substitute the acceptance of orthodox truths about him for personal allegiance to him and a ceaseless concern to be like him. Exultation in the sublime verities that form the Apostles' and the Nicene Creeds can subtly replace devotion to him who lives in the eternal Now.

Others there are who regard their Christian vocation as engagement in apocalyptic study. Their chief interest in the Bible is the guidance it gives them to foretell the future, especially the form and the time of Christ's coming again. Their specialty is to draft an eschatological map in which is charted the road to the holy city. They devote endless time to identifying the spots where the dragon and the great whore menace the highway, and they provide timetables of the events due to happen until the Lord comes. But the irony is that while they are masters of tomorrow, they are insensitive to today.

They are specialists on the direction, the byways, and the crossroads of the king's highway, but they never take this road themselves as pilgrims. They glory in being spectators with no interest whatever in being crusaders. They live comfortably and complacently with an air of pompous superiority. They are utterly insensitive to the biblical fact that the Lord Christ, who came yesterday and will come again tomorrow, is also here now as a contemporary presence. They ignore the fact that this Christ invites all who, like Peter, say to him, "I love you" and are responsive to his "Follow me," to take to the road with him in fellowship and in service today.

6. Theological Demonism

But there is something still more serious. I call it *theological demonism*. It is paradoxical but true that people can become so enthralled to "pure ideas," to "right opinions," that, in order to defend their position and to promote the cause of "orthodoxy" as they understand it, they violate God's moral order and fall prey to the demonic. They become fanaticized. Their honor is at stake. The traditional biblical enemy of truth and righteousness thereupon takes over. Contemporaneity is given to the figure of Satan in Milton's *Paradise Lost* and to the words he uttered: "Evil, be thou my good."

In recent times, Christian organizations in the United States and churches founded by American missions around the world have suffered defamation and disruption through the words and efforts of certain persons who exult in "orthodoxy." Those whom they attack they link to socialism, communism, or papal subversion. Their main support economically comes from wealthy Americans who dread what social reform might do to the "source of their gain." The new apostles stop at nothing, stoop to anything, resort to everything that will promote the cause of "orthodoxy," religious, social and political, as they understand it. Yet, despite their acclamation of the Bible and of Christ, they are betrayers of both. They are today's successors of people about whom the author of the letter to the Hebrews wrote, " . . . they crucify to themselves the Son of God afresh, and put him to an open shame . . ." "hold him up to contempt" (Heb. 6:6, K.J.V., R.S.V.). Their interest in people is to make them their tools. They do not follow the example of Christ, nor are they inspired by the Old Testament prophets and the spirit of Christ. Neither do they "care" like Christ for the human masses, for the hungry and oppressed.

While the influence of this militant demonism has now begun to wane in the United States, the callousness and cruelty that have marked its course in this country have gone overseas. Armed with clichés derogatory to the ecumenical movement, to the pursuit of social justice and the humanization of man, and even to evangelistic effort, apostles of hate and of antichrist move into the younger churches. They promote schism and decry efforts to establish Christian unity. As a result, some vital evangelical churches in Asia, Africa, and Latin America have been disrupted. But these schismatics will not prevail. The head of the church, who is not an idea but a reality, will have the last word. And that last word could be: " 'I was hungry and you gave me no food, I was thirsty and you gave me no drink, I was a stranger and you did not welcome me, naked and you did not clothe me, sick and in prison and you did not visit me . . . Truly I say to you, as you did it not to one of the least of these, you did it not to me.' And they will go away . . ." (Matt. 25:42–46).

With this we conclude the first facet of our study. As we recall reflectively the ground we have traversed, I can think of no words more appropriate to resound in our ears than those with which the apostle John concluded his first letter to Christians in his time: ". . . keep yourselves from idols" (1 John 5:21).

Chapter III

THE TRANSFORMING ENCOUNTER
&
THE IDOLATRY OF FEELING

The second facet of Christian reality is the reality of a personal relationship between human persons and the living God. This relationship is transforming in character and produces a new and creative type of personality. It is haunted, however, by the constant temptation to substitute feeling for reality. Just as ideas about God's revelation of himself and his purpose in history can take the place of personal faith in God and thereby become idols, so too, emotions relating to the human experience of God can become idols. There is an aesthetic idolatry just as there is an ideational idolatry. The claim to personal contact with God can involve mere appearance and not reality. Christian experience as both reality and appearance will be the theme of this chapter.

1. God-Man Encounter as Fact and Experience

It is a momentous happening when a man responds to God's quest for him and a personal relationship is established between the human self and Deity. Loving encounter is followed by conversation, reconciliation, prayer, new horizons, new life direction, new concerns, a new thrill in living, a new meaning to being "Christian." From being disdained as a pietistic cliché or just a theological conundrum, "conversion" takes on a fresh, dynamic significance. In the perspective of history, it stands out as a determinant of human destiny. Very significant in the annals of Protestantism and in the political annals of Western Europe and the United States is the fact that a young Frenchman, John Calvin, a devotee of Seneca the Stoic, was confronted, as was Saul of Tarsus, by a sovereign Lord. The artistic emblem called Calvin's Crest is art's abiding witness to what happened. An outstretched hand that holds a flaming heart is interpreted by these words, "My heart I give Thee, Lord, eagerly and sincerely."

In the Stoic tradition, as in much of the cold intellectualism that has marked both philosophy and theology in recent years, the heart and its profound significance for thought and life was ignored. But the heart, as the real center of being and the true home of the spirit, is being rediscovered and its importance is being emphasized. The timeless centrality in human nature of feeling, of sentiment, is being recognized in secular society. The development of psychiatric science in its multiple forms; the study of psychedelic phenomena and the yearning for an experience beyond the grounds of the material, the positivistic and the rational; the revolt of youth against the established order with an accompanying craving for meaning, for a cause, for a leader—these contemporary phenomena are evidence of the truth of what Pascal said: "The heart too has its reasons which Reason does not know."

Yes, "the heart too has its reasons." The truth is that it is a sentiment, an intuition, a longing of the heart, that provides the basis for the formulation of first principles and a philosophy of life, as suggested by F. H. Bradley, to whose viewpoint regarding feeling I referred in the preface to this study. As Pascal put it, "We know truth not only by the reason, but also by the heart, and it is in this last way that we know first principles" (*Pensées* 282).

Most significant also, as regards the relationship between heart and mind, between feelings and ideas, is Unamuno's famous book *The Tragic Sense of Life*. Reason cannot establish a sure intellectual basis for accepting the reality of God, but the heart can experience God's reality as a living presence with whom the soul can commune. Says the Spanish poet-philosopher—moving beyond his previous interpretation of religion as simply "struggle with God"—"I believe in God as I believe in my friends, because I feel the breath of his affection and his invisible and intangible hand that draws me, that guides me, that grasps me, because I have an intimate awareness of a special providence and of a universal mind that shapes my destiny" (*Del Sentimiento Trágico de la Vida*, p. 193, author's translation).

Here is a man who experienced the reality of God, who enjoyed communion with God, and who was also sensitive, more than any other man of letters in his time, to every phase of human thought and life. It is when we confront the reality of a man of God of this dimension that the words of Arnold Toynbee take on impressive significance: "Souls are greater than civilizations—civilizations are for souls." And human souls achieve the full dimension of their being when, and only when, they experience God as a loving, transforming, guiding presence. Herein is the reality of Christian sainthood—to be "God's men and women," as J. B. Phillips in his translation of the New Testament renders the word commonly translated "saints." In communion with God, "saints" become adjusted to God. And only through their leadership, as real souls, can civilizations too become adjusted to God, which they must do or perish.

In the perspective of the God-man encounter as a fact to be recognized, let us move on to consider encounter as *an experience to be examined*. Let us begin by considering the classical features that mark a personal relationship, vital communion, between man and God.

"Someone came to my soul." These words of one of the leading characters in Dostoevski's famous novel *The Brothers*

Karamazov crystallize in a classical manner the experience of God's coming into a human spirit. The young man who experienced the coming was never the same again. His changed life showed that he had become "God's man," an Eastern Orthodox saint. "Oh for more of God in my soul! Oh this pleasing pain!" So wrote in his diary, David Brainerd, a brilliant young intellectual who was ousted from Yale College in the mid-eighteenth century because of undue religious zeal. Ejected from Yale before graduation, Brainerd dedicated himself to live and work lovingly among primitive Indians of the Delaware Valley in Pennsylvania. God's presence in his soul did not make him comfortable or complacent. It rather created within him a passion to share more freely in the suffering and problems of those he called "my people."

Take another illustration. Listen to a stanza from a great Spanish lyric, the "Cántico Espiritual," of the sixteenth-century poet-mystic, John of the Cross.

> Reveal Thyself, I cry,
> E'en though the glory of Thy presence kill.
> For sick of love am I,
> And naught can cure my ill
> Save only if of Thee I have my fill.

The author of these lines was a passionate lover of God, of nature, and of man. The lines themselves were written in a prison cell in Toledo, Spain, where John of the Cross was confined. Why was he there? Because Father John manifested in his life and writings an heretical Christian ardor, a personal relationship to Deity not congenial to the cold ecclesiastical bureaucrats of his time. A simple comment is this. The most significant bond between the great Christian traditions and the multiple sects is something which all Christians need to pray for, rediscover, and promote—namely, the life of God in the soul of man. Only then can the quest for Christian unity move beyond appearance to reality.

But now the question arises, How does God come to the soul? What are the preconditions for an experience of his presence in life's "daily round and common task"? The most basic and classical answer to this question is found in the book of Isaiah. Said the great prophet of Israel's exile: "Have you not known? Have you not heard? The LORD is the everlasting God, the Creator of the ends of the earth. He does not faint or grow weary, his understanding is unsearchable. He gives power to the faint, and to him who has no might he increases strength. Even youths shall faint and be weary, and young men shall fall exhausted; but they who wait for the LORD [who take God seriously] shall renew their strength [shall exchange their strength for God's strength], they shall mount up with wings like eagles, they shall run and not be weary, they shall walk and not faint" (Isa. 40:28–31).

The meaning is plain. God is questing. The total failure of human resources should not be the occasion for fed-upness or despair nor for the cessation of all effort. But the goal of man's effort must be different. It must be a concentration of energy upon his proud ego to compel it to give God a chance, to allow God to enter into the innermost chamber of his being. When this happens, when the "everlasting God" who "does not faint or grow weary" and whose "understanding is unsearchable" is "waited for" and takes over, a new era begins in human experience. Man's flagging energy is transformed into divine strength. When he becomes "God's man" he is caught by a rapturous elation and soars aloft like an eagle, liberated from the trammels that enthralled him. He will become enthusiastically dedicated to a cause and will speed like an athlete towards the goal of its realization. And when the rapture and the race are over, he will be able to settle down quietly to a walking pace, bearing witness to what God continues to be to him and to do for him, even when the going is rough.

It is possible, however, to be still more specific as to how

God comes to the soul. There is a beyond to the basic precondition for God's coming, namely, that the human spirit shall reach the point of submission to his entrance and control. God, in his quest for man, is no mere patient vigilante who awaits the appropriate moment for taking control. He is an active participant in preparing the soul for the great encounter in which he will take over with the soul's complete acquiescence. This leads us to consider two classical types of prelude to the spiritual occurrence which has been poetically expressed in these words: "He is mine, and I am His. And we are one forever."

One type of prelude to the God-given encounter is quiet and undramatic. The other is dramatic and sonorous.

2. *Forms of Spiritual Encounter*

There have been instances in Christian biography when men and women of great spiritual stature and creative influence could not tell the circumstance, the day, or even the year, when God first became real to them and Christ became dear to them. They had no memory of a specific conversion experience. A notable illustration of this fact is found in the life of John Livingstone, a famous Scottish minister of the seventeenth century. Here is the paradox. Livingstone, when twenty-seven years of age, preached a sermon to thousands of people gathered in the open air in Lanarkshire County in the environs of Glasgow, during a traditional Scottish communion season. Some years later, when a study was made of the fruits of that sermon, it was discovered that 500 people attributed to it their conversion. Paradoxically, however, the preacher himself, according to his own autobiography, was unaware of the precise occasion or period in his boyhood years when God first became a living reality for him. Brought up in a warmly evangelical home, he had, as Paul's young colleague Timothy may have done, passed quietly and undramatically into the experience of God's redemptive presence.

But it has not been so with the majority of those who are more than nominally Christian. Drama in some form or another has been part of their experience of becoming a "new creation." Many of diverse backgrounds and in the most varied types of environment have experienced the pangs derived from an awareness of sinful behavior. They have seen themselves in a new light. Rumblings of discontent sound within them. They have been suddenly awakened from their complacency. Like the denizens of the city of Mansoul in John Bunyan's "Holy War," they tremble at the detonation of the "battering rams of Boanerges." Eventually, however, despite the resistance of Diabolus and his kin, the city falls to the troops of Prince Emmanuel.

The dramatic movement from conviction of sin to salvation, and the soul's subsequent struggle with evil, is presented by Bunyan in different imagery in his greater work *The Pilgrim's Progress*. Mansoul is personalized in the figure of a single person, a man called Christian, who has become a pilgrim. Weighted down by an overwhelming sense of sin—symbolized by a heavy burden on his back which he cannot unfetter—the pilgrim comes, in the course of his journey, to a highway "fenced on either side with a Wall . . . called *Salvation*." Running upwards, "burdened *Christian*" reaches a place where "stood a *Cross*, and a little below in the bottom, a Sepulchre." The author continues,

> So I saw in my Dream, that just as *Christian* came up with the *Cross*, his burden loosed from off his Shoulders, and fell from off his back, and began to tumble; and so continued to do, till it came to the mouth of the Sepulchre, where it fell in, and I saw it no more.
>
> Then was *Christian* glad and lightsome, and said with a

merry heart, *He hath given me rest, by his sorrow; and life, by his death.*

Then *Christian* gave three leaps for joy, and went on singing.

Thus far did I come loaden with my sin,
Nor could ought ease the grief that I was in,
Till I came hither: . . .
Blest Cross! blest Sepulchre! blest rather be
The Man that there was put to shame for me.

The experience here delineated of spiritual liberation and rapturous joy, both related historically and existentially to Jesus Christ, crucified and risen, constitutes the subjective core of Christian reality. In New Testament language, the meaningfulness of which has been confirmed through the ages in diverse cultures down to this revolutionary time, the Man of Bethlehem and Galilee, of Golgotha and Olivet, continues to live in those who have made their commitment to him and live their lives for him and for the kingdom that will come through him. "I have been crucified with Christ," said the man who on the Damascus highway encountered the crucified, risen Nazarene; "it is no longer I who live, but Christ who lives in me" (Gal. 2:20).

Never did these words of Paul have more challenge and relevancy than in this time of secular crusaders who seek a new society in which justice and human rights will have the central place and races and nations will be reconciled. To experience Christ in the full dimension of Christian reality is to be possessed by Christ's passion for people, for their souls and also for their bodies, for their relationship to God and to one another. And this is possible because "if anyone is in Christ, he is a new creation," in the world and for the world. For Christian experience in this dimension is inseparably related to an abiding sensitivity to these other words of Paul which he addressed to Christians in the Greek city of Corinth, "God was in Christ reconciling the world to himself . . . So we are ambassadors for Christ, God making his appeal through us. We beseech you on behalf of Christ, be reconciled to God" (2 Cor. 5:17-20).

In order that their "ambassadorial" role might be effectively fulfilled, Christians on the Day of Pentecost received, in accordance with Christ's promise, the baptism of the Holy Spirit. The presence of the Holy Spirit in the life of Christians, with all that it signifies by way of spiritual power and which in some instances is accompanied by visible charismatic phenomena such as speaking in tongues and the gift of healing, is a part of Christian reality in its experiential dimension. For more than fifty years what is currently known as the Pentecostal Movement has been growing in influence and prestige and today is making an impact within Roman Catholicism and in the churches of historic Protestantism. This movement calls for very serious study. What does it mean to be "filled with the Spirit" in reality and in appearance in the twentieth century?

To this issue we will return in the next chapter. Meanwhile, let us not forget this fact. The same voice that has sounded through the ages addresses our generation. It says: "Seek God who is seeking you. Receive his forgiveness, experience his love, live in his fellowship, receive the gift of the Holy Spirit; share your experience with others; move together towards the City."

3. When Emotions Become Idols

With this we pass once again from reality to appearance. Our study of a personal relationship to God as an integral facet of Christian reality has a tragic epilogue. Just as ideas about God can become substitutes for the personal awareness of God's reality, so an emotion, expressive of some form of religious experience but not necessarily involving meaningful contact with God, can become a substitute for a personal relationship with God and devotion to him. Religious emotions, like theological ideas, can become ends to themselves. When this happens, emotions become idols. Ceasing to be the creative instruments and spiritual accompaniments of a God-man friendship, they become psychological agents of a man-God divinization. When this happens, what alleges to be Christian experience manifests itself as subjective ingrownness and dedication to aesthetic thrills. In a very subtle and paradoxical manner, the love of religious feeling can take the place of the love of God.

Let me clarify this paradox. Feeling is central in human nature. It is both the inward source of ideologies and the outward expression of a spiritual mood. An experience of God is and should be linked to deep emotion, whether this emotion be expressed quietly or loudly, visibly or invisibly. It is nevertheless true that in religion feeling can be subtly exalted as the thing to be cultivated and made manifest, thus becoming an idol, a subjective substitute for reality.

What can happen is this. In certain instances to be actively Christian becomes equated with religious loquacity, with endless talk about things having to do with religion. The tongue takes over, assuming spiritual lordship. The peril of this type of lordship is stressed both in the Old Testament and in the New. In one of the Hebrew Psalms, we read this expression of concern about endless talk. "May the Lord cut off all flattering lips, the tongue that makes great boasts, those who say, 'With our tongue we will prevail, our lips are with us; Who is our master?'" (Ps. 12:3, 4). Said the Apostle James, "The tongue is a little member and boasts of great things. How great a forest is set ablaze by a small fire! And the tongue is a fire" (James 3:5, 6).

A classic paradigm of the tongue and its activity as an emotional idol is found in *The Pilgrim's Progress*. This Christian classic has already provided us with a dramatic illustration of spiritual rebirth. Here is the polar opposite of spirituality. Christian and his companion, Faithful, on their journey to the City come upon a fellow traveler called Talkative. Faithful was entranced by the man's fascinating conversation. But Christian cautioned him remarking that their new companion, who was the son of a man called Saywell and whose home was in Prating Row, was " . . . notwithstanding his fine tongue . . . a sorry fellow." He informed Faithful that Talkative had no place for religion "in his heart, house, or conversation," that "his Religion is to make noise therewith."

"He talketh of Prayer, of Repentance, of Faith, and of the New-Birth," Christian continued, "but he knows but only to talk of them . . . *A Saint abroad, and a Devil at home* . . . if he finds in any of [his sons] *a foolish timorousness,* (for so he calls the first appearance of a tender conscience) he calls them fools and blockheads." In his business relations he "will go beyond . . . defraud, beguile, and over-reach" the men he deals with. And then in the tradition of Puritanism and of Christian piety at their best, Christian stresses the fact that "The Soul of Religion is the practick part," that true religion involves concern for people in need, and that it is to be judged by the *fruit* it bears and not by the talk it makes. He thereupon suggested to Faithful that he raise with Talkative, who had told him he was eager for more conversation, the question of *"the power of Religion."*

Faithful phrased his question in these terms: *"How doth the saving Grace of God discover it self, when it is in the heart of man?"* Replied Talkative, *"Where the Grace of God is in the heart, it causeth a great out-cry against sin."* To which Faithful responded, *"I think you should rather say, It shows it self by inclining the Soul to abhor its sin."* Talkative was ruffled, and contended, "Why, what difference is there between crying out against, and abhoring of sin?" "Oh! a great deal," said Faithful, *"a man may cry out against sin, of policy;*

but he cannot abhor it, but by vertue of a godly antipathy against it."

Could any words be more pertinent to the religious situation today? How many professional talkers there are these days in churches and homes, in business and government, who holler and storm against what is sinful and wrong as they conceive it, but who do so only "of policy." That is to say, it is in their interest and in the interests of their group and perhaps their nation to anathematize certain things that are being said or done by people they dislike. They are anti-, anti-, anti-, Super-antis. Yet they are themselves utterly insensitive to the presence of anything amiss or sinful in their own sentiment and behavior. They may be churchmen, but they are sub-Christian and can be even sub-human.

Talkative made another try to answer Faithful's question regarding "*a discovery of a work of grace in the heart.*" His second reply was, "*Great knowledge of Gospel Mysteries.*" To which Faithful made this response: "*A man may know like an Angel, and yet be no Christian . . . to know, is a thing that pleaseth Talkers and Boasters; but to do, is that which pleaseth God.*"

As emphasized earlier, it is one thing to know the truth and quite another thing to do the truth. And Christian truth is inseparably related to life and action. In Christians, as in Christ, the word "must become flesh." But Talkative, bitterly resentful of the suggestion that he lacked both conviction of sin and true spiritual understanding, chimed in with the words, "You lie at the catch again; this is not for edification"—which for him meant edification for deceit! It was the judgment of Talkative that Faithful's approach to the problem of man and the meaning of "true religion" was not conducive to "building up" the existing structure, but was a menace to the whole edifice. How germane this is to our way of life!

After Christian had heartily commended his fellow pilgrim for the manner of his approach to Talkative, whom he described as one of "these Talkative Fools . . . [who] puzzle the World, blemish Christianity, and grieve the sincere," Faithful burst into poetry:

How Talkative *at first lifts up his Plumes!*
How bravely doth he speak! how he presumes
To drive down all before him! but so soon
As Faithful *talks of* Heart-work, *like the Moon*
That's past the full, into the wain he goes;
And so will all, but he that Heart-work *knows.*

Let us take note: "heart-work." "Heart-work" there must be, if "holy living" is to be more than appearance.

A second aberration in the realm of religious feeling emerges when a person becomes emotionally committed to the realization of a religious pattern. The formal pursuit of a specific pattern of religious living can become one's spiritual ultimate. I vividly remember an illustration of this type of aberration in the life of a student who attended Princeton Theological Seminary. During one of the seminary sessions, back in the forties, I became bombarded with complaints by many seminarians regarding the abnormal behavior of a first-year student from California. The young man in question wore on his coat lapel a very garish button of which he always seemed very conscious and to which he sought in diverse ways to attract the attention of his fellow students. Whenever one of them would ask for a close look at the adornment and inquire what words were engraven upon it, this would happen: With an air of marked superiority the snobbish button-wearer would reply, "It says, 'Are you saved?'"

In an environment where everyone took it for granted that he was "saved," or at least that no one had the right to challenge his spiritual estate, the situation became so tense that a group of students brought their grievance to the President! I asked the California youth to come to see me. We had a long, interesting talk together. He opened up to me his past. He told me that he had been brought up in a very rigid and isolated sect of which his parents were members. A requirement of the sect was that every person belonging to it should confront outsiders with whom he came in contact with the same query, "Are you saved?" At this point, the young lad broke down and said to me, "Doctor, I have to confess to you that I don't know what these words mean. But I was obliged to address them to others out of loyalty to my parents and to the group." He then admitted dejectedly that he had never had a "salvation" experience of his own, and that a personal relationship to God meant nothing to him! Following subsequent talks together, this lad and I agreed that his confusion and immaturity were such that he should return home and rethink his whole life and vocation.

The encounter with this youth was a very moving and illuminating experience. It led to much pondering. The case provides a primitive but basic illustration of the fact that there can be, and are, people in the Christian tradition at all levels for whom to be Christian means the dedication of one's self to the realization of a prescribed pattern. The pattern may take diverse forms, but its loyal and active acceptance becomes life's ultimate imperative.

For a sophisticated illustration of this type of spiritual commitment, let me move from the realm of sectarian fanaticism to the world of high churchism. One of the most intriguing books I have read in recent years is the biographical study *Cosmo Gordon Lang*, by J. G. Lockhart. Lang was for many years Archbishop of Canterbury, the predecessor in that office of a man of a totally different temperament, William Temple.

One evening, while riding with a friend in the Downs of Wiltshire County in England, young Gordon Lang, a recent Oxford University graduate dreaming of a political career, was suddenly gripped by a new question about which he speaks in his diary: "As the horses were walking down the slope in the setting sun, a question unbidden, wholly irrelevant to anything that had previously entered my thoughts, shot itself into my mind—'After all, why shouldn't *you* be ordained?'" As Lang pondered the question, his thoughts moved thus: "Why on earth *should* I be ordained? . . . I had no sort of religious experience to justify the question." When he asked a distinguished Anglican clergyman, Scott Holland, "what signs a perplexed man ought to have of any real vocation to Holy Orders," and Holland replied, " a love of souls," Lang's comment was, "I could not understand his language." But, not long thereafter, ordination ceased to be a question and became a "command" that thundered in his ear. So the young Oxford don prepared himself for the ministry and was ordained.

Yet the basic issue remained and became intensified as the new minister moved up the ecclesiastical ladder and finally became an archbishop, first of York and then of Canterbury. What did it mean to be a clergyman, and in particular an archbishop? What should be his attitude towards people, towards Christ, towards himself? What image, what life pattern, should be his ideal and the goal of his aspiring if he were to fulfill his destiny in the sight of man and in every human situation? These questions remained. As for people, Cosmo Gordon Lang never got close to them, nor they to him. In a letter to his mother he wrote once, "It is not the preaching that tires, it is the strain of men." He would not say, like Sartre, "Hell is other people," but other people were a veritable strain to him.

As regards Jesus Christ, it was not until late in life that Lang began to become aware of him as a living reality beyond the Eucharist and the Apostolic succession. Very moving and significant are words he wrote in his summer home in the

Scottish Highlands on the eve of his sixtieth birthday: "I come burdened with the thought of manifold failure. I have been letting myself down." He feels himself to be like the prodigal son, returning home to his father. But he is convinced that behind his early experience in the Wiltshire Downs "there is a reality—God in Christ. I must stake my life on that truth." Then in penitent mood and looking toward the end of his career, the Archbishop movingly exclaimed, "It is all I have really to live for, so I must simply get back to it, rebuild these few remaining years on it, be reconverted and trust that even yet I may be able out of the fragments left to give God a love, a life, which has not actually failed for his purpose." What this means is that an archbishop had been living in appearance and wished to return to reality.

Lang's life concern had been not what it was to be a Christian and act like a Christian, but rather what it meant to be a church hierarch and look like one in all that he said and did. The resulting paradox was that the Archbishop rarely seemed to be the same person. Each occasion on which a friend saw him he looked like a different person, and even at intervals on the same occasion. Says his biographer, "At the dinner table, for example, a click could almost be heard as one Lang went off and another came on." Symbolic of this "strangely unintegrated person, a jangle of warring personalities which never reached a working agreement among themselves," is the remark of the great English painter, Sir William Orpen, who had been invited to paint the Archbishop's portrait. As he concentrated his gaze upon the figure he was designated to reproduce on canvas, the artist exclaimed, "I see seven Archbishops. Which one of them am I to paint?" It is one thing for a person to be his own true self in the most diverse situations because of his commitment to be a real man; it is a wholly other thing for him to be diverse selves in the same situation because of commitment to a professional image.

4. The Tragedy of Christian Nominalism

Let me bring to a close this facet of our study by alluding to the most common type of substitute for a vital experience of God and communion with him. It takes the form of identifying what it means to be Christian with being personally present at a Christian service of public worship. Now let it be quite clear that the public worship of God is an integral part of Christian reality in its communal dimension. But it is a tragic, sociological fact that a very large proportion of those who are present at "solemn assemblies" are not there because they take God seriously. They are not there as true worshippers. They are there for two other reasons. Some are there because they seek and receive an emotional thrill. Others are there because their presence in the sanctuary from time to time helps them to maintain an image and fulfill a pattern which they cherish, both for psychological and public reasons. They regard themselves, and are regarded by others, as "Christians," though they are so only in name—in appearance, but not in reality. This is a major problem of contemporary Christianity. Membership in an institution called the church becomes in the life of many millions of people a substitute for a personal relationship to God and for effective membership in the family of God.

This phenomenon of Christian nominalism is rampant across all ecclesiastical boundaries. Prevalent for generations in churches belonging to the Roman and Orthodox traditions, it has now become a growing characteristic of the churches of historical Protestantism. For that reason, membership in the latter tends to be outstripped in progressive growth and spiritual vitality by the so-called "sects," especially by the Pentecostal churches.

In Roman Catholic circles today, due to the influence of Pope John XXIII, the Second Vatican Council, and the rediscovery of the Bible, creative change is taking place. When a question was recently addressed to an eminent theologian of the Roman Catholic Church in Chile, "Sir, what do you consider to be the main problem of your church today?" his reply was, "We Catholics must make Christians." Traditionally, especially following the Council of Trent, the only thing that mattered was willingness to accept the appellation "Catholic." In Latin America it was not uncommon to hear one say, "I am an atheist, but I am a Catholic."

The time has come for Protestants around the world to say, "We Protestants must make Christians." The multitude of people who are church members only for the sake of status, or who attend church services in quest of aesthetic thrills from sound or symbol and nothing more, or who are church "alumni" who appear in old pews on the dates dictated by the calendar as being historically significant—all these devotees of Christian nominalism need to discover, as individual persons, what it means to be Christian, not merely by appellation, but in truth.

This discovery can only be made when the human spirit, in quest of a new life and craving to be released from the fetters that bind it to its old self-centered ego, surrenders without reservation to him, Jesus Christ, who is the Savior and Lord of life. This is not religious romanticism; it is spiritual reality. The words that changed the life of a brilliant young man of the fourth century, Augustine, who was struggling with the problem of sexual unchastity and had the habit of praying, "Oh, God, give me chastity, but not now," can solve the major problem of contemporary man. Here are the words that produced change in the young North African: " . . . put on the Lord Jesus Christ." These were the words of the man from Tarsus (Rom. 13:14) by which he meant: "Let Christ wrap up your whole being like a cloak. Let him be your armor against sensual proddings that allure you." To be "wrapped" in Christ in this manner, to "know the love of Christ which surpasses knowledge," is to be "Christ's man" and to be "filled with all the fulness of God" (Eph. 3:19). Amid the new quest for meaning and a cause, in both church and society, the words of that pre-Renaissance Spanish missionary-scholar, the Majorcan, Raymond Lull, take on contemporary relevance: "I have one passion in life and it is He."

So, too, do the words of that Presbyterian Scotsman, Samuel Rutherford, Principal of St. Andrews University, who wrote from a prison cell where he was confined for religious and political reasons, "I am sending you this letter from Christ's Palace in Aberdeen." In this dungeon he enjoyed the Presence. He knew what it meant to bear Christ's cross and to "share the fellowship of Christ's suffering." In this era of revolution and suffering, the cross and the crucified take on fresh creative meaning for all who seek a new world of reality.

Profoundly significant also in this revolutionary time are the words of Blaise Pascal, "Christ will be in agony till the end of the world" (*Mystère de Jésus*). Why? Because, as Søren Kierkegaard, another profound interpreter of Christian reality, expressed the same paradox, "Perfect love is perfect sorrow." Love and sorrow are inseparable companions, and will be to the journey's close.

Chapter IV

THE COMMUNITY OF CHRIST

CHURCHISM

We now come to the communal expression of Christian reality.

While the human person is a spiritual ultimate, and the individual Christian is a constitutive part of Christian reality, there is no place for individualism as a human ultimate. Each individual person for whom Jesus Christ is a supreme spiritual reality is under obligation to Christ and to himself to become related to others who profess the same ultimate loyalty. He thereby becomes a member of a community, a "fellowship of men and women for whom Jesus Christ is Lord." The Christian church, when true to its nature, is a community of Christ, formed by people who are friends of Christ and of one another. That is to say, in its ultimate essence, the church is *communal* and not structural. Some structure, of course, the community must have if its members are to take their identity seriously as friends of Him who said, "You are my friends if you do what I command you" (John 15:14). Individually and corporately, it is theirs to obey the mandate of Christ, who is both friend and Lord and who, with them and through them as a local or worldwide community of devoted followers, will achieve God's purpose in the world. Structure is for achievement.

It is important to delineate the specific quality of Christian friendship as a loving, meaningful, dynamic force. It is friendship on the road, with a goal in mind. Christians, like all humans, enjoy, and should enjoy, having a good time together. But they are more than a fraternity elite. Christian friendship has a beyond. The Italian author Papini, one of the countless biographers of Jesus, spoke thus of the home of Jesus, "Jesus' home," he said, "was the road along which he walked with his friends in search of new friends." Beyond the encounters between Jesus and his friends which are associated with the Palestinian highways and byways, with the Upper Room, with Golgotha and the empty tomb, with the Galilean seaside and Mount Olivet, the Day of Pentecost brought together thousands of people. Through the work of the Holy Spirit and a Spirit-inspired sermon by Christ's once-wayward friend Simon Peter, those people became a new society of friends, the Christian church. The reality of friendship in the newly formed community made itself manifest in the awareness of a common relationship to Christ as Savior and Lord. It appeared in the breakdown of racial and linguistic barriers, and in the creation of enthusiasm, through the presence of the Holy Spirit. It produced also the love of gatherings for fellowship and worship, in homes and in the Temple, following the redistribution of money and material things among the members of the new community.

In these happenings on the Day of Pentecost when the community of Christ came into being, we have the establishment of a timeless representative pattern of what Christians should be and do as members of the new community called the church, the ecclesia. *Ecclesia*, the term used in the Hellenistic tradition to designate the persons publicly elected to represent the citizenry of a Greek town, was adopted by the Christian community to identify themselves, not as members of a civic or national community, but as the representatives of God's new humanity.

1. Biblical Images of the Church

In quest of what constitutes the essential nature of the Christian church as the community of Christ, the new humanity, let us glance briefly at four basic images used by New Testament writers to portray what constituted for them the "Israel of God" (Gal. 6:16), that is, the "New Israel," the "household of faith" (Gal. 6:10). Each of these images suggests traits which should characterize the life of the Christian community when true to its own nature. A study of them will help us grasp the essential biblical meaning of the Christian church.

There is first the image of a *flock*, a figure common to the Old Testament and the New. The best known and most loved Psalm in the Old Testament begins thus: "The LORD is my shepherd" (Ps. 23). In the New Testament, Christ is the shepherd; Christians are his sheep. What does this signify? In the perspective of biblical usage and Oriental life, *mutual sensitivity* is at the core of the shepherd-sheep relationship. The shepherd loves his sheep. He leads them to the most fruitful pastures. He knows each one of them by name. When a member of the flock goes astray, the shepherd goes in search of it and is willing to die in the quest. The sheep on their part recognize the shepherd's voice; they are responsive to his call; they follow him wherever he leads them.

The second image of the church is that of a *building*. Now a building, when its foundations are secure and strong (Luke 6:48), is the symbol of *stability*. The house built upon a rock can, in the words of Jesus, stand the roughest assaults of wind and weather (Matt. 7:25). In his sublime letter to the Ephesians, which is the climax of his thinking, Paul presents the "household of God" as a building in which God dwells, a "holy temple." The foundation of this building is the apostles and prophets; its cornerstone is Christ. The walls of the building, as another apostolic author declares, are composed of "living stones." These stones are the saints, Christ's men and women, who grow up together into a "spiritual house" (1 Peter 2:5). It is a striking fact that in the New Testament imagery of the church as a building, stability involves the following basic features: continuity with the apostles and prophets, the centrality of Christ, the abiding presence of God, and the vitality and growth of the individual components of the structure. There is no mere glorying in what was or is, but in what is *becoming*. This building, if we take the symbolism seriously, is presented not as a static but as a living structure which is grounded in the past, allied to the eternal, and vibrating in the present. It is not a monument to what has been, a memory of yesterday that is past, but an image of a reality that is and must be.

Now comes the third image. It is the figure of a *bride*. This is a universal human image that transcends all ages and cultures, that moves beyond the rural and the industrial, the urban and the suburban. This biblical image of the "people of God," the community of Christ, as a bride symbolizes *loyalty* —loyalty to the person to whom one has become betrothed. Involved in this loyalty is love's deepest emotion, jubilation at the thought of wedlock, abiding expectancy that the great day of union will come, and dedication to getting ready for the event. In using this image, Paul stresses Christ's passionate love of the church as his bride (Eph. 5:24) for whom he sacrificed his whole life as a means for the purification of his betrothed.

The great apocalyptic event toward which the church is represented as moving, and history's climactic moment, is the "marriage of the Lamb" (Rev. 19:6–8). By this event, the community of Christ, the new humanity, is finally united to Christ and lives beyond the boundary of space and time and all the powers of sin and Satan. As "the Bride, the wife of the Lamb," the Christian community becomes "the holy city Jerusalem coming down out of heaven from God" (Rev. 21: 9 f.). In this final apocalyptic vision of the Bride is symbolized the consummation of "holy history," the union of God and the redeemed community in such a way that religious symbols represented by the temple pass away. In the new city of God, symbolized by the church as Christ's bride, there is no temple structure. Says the Seer, " . . . its temple is the Lord God the Almighty and the Lamb. And the city has no need of sun or moon to shine upon it, for the glory of God is its light and its lamp is the Lamb" (Rev. 21:22 f.).

In the eventual union of Christ and the church, the temple as the historic structural symbol of God's presence will be no more. His luminous reality focused in the Lamb as its medium will be everywhere present. This fact raises a question which cannot be summarily dismissed. Should not the assumption be taken seriously that as the community of Christ faces its apocalyptic tomorrow, visible symbols of the place where God is met and the objects associated with his presence will and should have increasingly less significance in the church's life? Should they not be replaced by a sense of the real presence of Christ in every facet of Christian living? This, of course, raises the whole question of the status of symbolism in the sanctuary and in worship.

We now come to that image of the church which gives expression, in the most comprehensive and dynamic way, to the church's nature and status. The community of Christ is the *body* of Christ. Christ is the head; members of the community are the body. In the biological reality of the human body are epitomized the essential qualities of the church as flock, building, and bride. A true body, that is, the organism which is inseparably associated with the human person, gives concrete expression to the three traits just described: sensitivity, stability, and loyalty. These traits mark respectively the mutual responsiveness in sheep-shepherd relations, the firmness of an edifice constructed on secure foundations, and the loving fealty of a woman pledged to matrimony.

But the body moves beyond all these traits. It is the supreme expression of *functional mobility*. The function of a body, the reason and ground of its existence, is to cultivate the

health and achieve the strength that is needed if it is to respond to the mandate of the head, if it is to undertake the
specific activity decided upon by the mind. No human body
can be true to its nature or fulfill its destiny as a physiological
entity if it exists merely for the promotion of its own health,
strength, or beauty. A man's or a woman's body is truly their
body when it carries out their will in action—when, coordi-
nating the activity of all its diverse members, it becomes the
instrument for the execution of a task or the achievement of
a goal. In the fulfillment of its ultimate function, the body
may have to suffer or even die and be buried. But whatever
the consequences of the corporeal action undertaken, a human body proves true to itself when it marshals all its energies
to obey the mind that directs it and to which it mysteriously
belongs. The role of the body is to be a servant. If therefore,
this biblical image is taken seriously, the church, as the body
of Christ, is true to him and to itself when it exists as Christ's
servant. For that reason, the functional mobility of the body
as a servant is consonant with the spirit of the Bible and basic
to the loyal service of him who said, "You are my friends if
you do what I command you" (John 15:14). And Jesus Christ
as supreme commander continues, through the Holy Spirit, to
summon to action and to guide "the church, which is his
body" (Eph. 1:22 f.).

To take this analogy seriously is to remember, of course,
that no human flesh is perfect. There are physical imperfections in the body, and as the years advance, ailments tend to
multiply. The Christian church as the body of Christ, while
being a society of Christ's friends, is also, as its members
recognize or should recognize, a society of sinners. Of this
fact the chief friend is realistically aware and is concerned
about it. For that reason, the members and leaders of the
community of Christ in its local, national, and world dimension should always take care never to disguise the fact of the
church's imperfections. Nothing proves more disastrous than

when a church, whether a small sectarian group or a huge ecclesiastical establishment, conceals its sins, avows its theological and liturgical perfection, or glories in its power. When this happens—when a Christian church proudly seeks to draw attention to itself, when it is unwilling to "take the form of a servant" and to obey a contemporary mandate of its head, when it is vainly concerned to become a complacent showpiece—disaster is in the offing.

A Christian pastor was visiting the home of a woman whose husband had died the previous day. He entered the room where the dead body was lying. The mortician had done a marvelous job on the corpse. Said the minister to the widow, "You know, he never looked better in his life!" This is a parable. A church body can look wonderful and be dead. The aesthetic beauty of an ecclesiastical corpse can receive more acclaim than the corporation's common life. Let the body of Christ today take to the road in obedience to its head. Let it, when circumstances require, joyously elect to live an uncouth life of service for God and people. For uncouth life is better than aesthetic death.

2. The Functional Role of the Church as the Body of Christ

We are now ready to move forward to consider the functional role of the body of Christ. Taking seriously the image of the body as the metaphor that furnishes Christian thought with the most biblical and dynamic concept of the purpose for which the corporate Christian community exists in the world, let us concentrate our attention upon the church's role.

One of the many insights of John Calvin into Christian reality is enshrined in these words: "The Christian church is the instrument of God's glory." It is the medium through which God unveils in history the splendor of his character and the nature of his purpose for mankind. The church as the body of Christ is God's servant. To the church is committed the task of pursuing this double objective, namely, to unveil to man the splendor of God's character and to achieve in man the advent of a new humanity. Recognition of the church's role as being essentially instrumental, that of a servant, is absolutely indispensable for a true understanding of the church's nature and of the responsibility that belongs to all churches and church members everywhere.

To be true to the church as the community of Christ, it is incumbent upon Christians that they come together from time to time to worship God corporately and to enjoy fellowship. Where they gather, whether in a great cathedral or in a simple hall, in an apartment living room or in an underground cellar, does not affect the essence of Christian worship. The form of service in which they engage, whether highly liturgical or of Quaker simplicity, whether conducted by an episcopal functionary or by a simple layman, is not determinative of genuine Christian worship. What matters is not appearance, but reality. And Christian reality in worship involves the spirit of him who conducts the worship service and the spirit of those who participate in it. It is important to remember that in the Bible the "worship of God" and the "service of God" are inseparably related. Christian worship involves the response of the worshipper to God, to God's claims upon his whole being, in such a way that he gives his entire selfhood to God as a sacrificial offering. In doing so, he gives expression to a basic facet of the priesthood of all believers. Very cogent at this point are these words of the Apostle Paul: "I appeal to you therefore, brethren, by the mercies of God, to present your bodies as a living sacrifice, holy and acceptable to God, which is your spiritual worship" (Rom. 12:1).

The most enlightening and moving definition of Christian worship with which I am acquainted was phrased by a twentieth-century saint, J. H. Oldham, in these terms: "Worship is the response of believing men in adoration and joyous self-dedication to God's revelation of himself and to his redeeming grace" *(The Church and Its Function in Society)*. The point is here made that we worship God when, with minds enlightened as to what God has done for us, we dedicate ourselves to him with full abandon in prayer and in praise. Worship is thus not an emotional thrill that we seek, but an emotional response that we make. The former is appearance; the latter is reality.

So, too, with the sacraments which are symbolic accompaniments of Christian worship. Baptism, when truly meaningful, is the receipt by a believing Christian of water sprinkled upon him, or in which he is immersed, in the name of Jesus Christ. It is for him the seal of his personal response to Christ as his cleanser from sin. The Lord's Supper, or, as it is designated in some Christian circles, Holy Communion or the Eucharist, is the acceptance by a Christian of bread and wine as symbols of Christ's body and blood that were sacrificed for him. These elements, when received believingly in fellowship with other Christians, are accompanied, not within them but through them, by the reality of Jesus Christ himself as a real presence.

When Baptism and the Lord's Supper, however, are given the status of spiritual realities in their own right, whose influence is automatic and unrelated to the spiritual mood of the person who receives them, they become churchly idols. In such a case, allegiance to these sacraments takes the place of allegiance to Christ as man's Savior from sin and the source of his life. When, moreover, it is affirmed that the administration of Baptism and the Lord's Supper is the exclusive prerogative of ministers and that at no time and under no circumstances does an ordinary lay Christian have the right to baptize or to administer the Lord's Supper, a situation is created in which certain members of Christ's body make decisions that are the sole right of him who is the head. When, also, a particular form of traditional order or of worship becomes the ultimate for the direction of all church affairs, men appointed to be Christ's servants can become his masters, ignoring new situations and becoming insensitive to the onward march of the Lord.

But let it not be forgotten that Christian worship, when conducted in public by the community of Christ, involves the preaching of the Word. Members of the community must not only speak to God, receive the sacramental symbols of God's presence, and give themselves to God. They must, also and above all, listen to God. It is the responsibility of the person chosen by the community to be their pastor and teacher to open up to God's people for their spiritual growth and witness, the full dimension of God's self-disclosure of himself as presented in Holy Scripture. This will involve giving vocal expression to the centrality of Christ and the gospel, and to the abiding reality of the Holy Spirit, in the context of the times.

This leads us to the second functional responsibility of the Christian church as the body of Christ. Worship must move to *witness*. Unreserved dedication to God must lead to total involvement in the work of God. This must be done by a prophetic confrontation of human reality, by missionary zeal, and by the pursuit of Christian unity.

God, let the church never forget, is at work in the world for which he cares. It is therefore the responsibility of Christians, individually and collectively, to set the life of man in its contemporary context in the light of God. This involves an enlightened Christian understanding of what is happening in the world, sensitivity to what God is doing and desires to be done. It also involves an awareness of the presence and work of demonic forces and of the goals which these forces are pursuing.

A prophetic confrontation by Christians of the present-day world has much to learn from the Hebrew prophets, especially from Jeremiah. Of profound inspiration also, and of great relevance for Christian social concern today, is John Calvin's interpretation of the role of the State in human affairs. "The State," said Calvin, "is God's vice-regent to maintain humanity among men." Here is the ultimate law by which a government or a social order must be judged. Does a given political system or a current social structure make it possible for people to be truly human and to enjoy a humane existence as God's creatures and the object of his concern? If not, Christians, as responsible citizens, are confronted with a challenge to do something about it and to explore the meaning of justice and social change in the context of Scripture and the contemporary situation.

Missionary zeal is an equally essential part of Christian witness. This signifies involvement in Christ's mission in the world. It means that Christians must proclaim the gospel of Christ by speech, spoken and written, and also by the lives they live and the things they do. Evangelism, the proclamation of the gospel by lip and pen, is an abiding responsibility of the community of Christ. With passionate conviction, crystalline clarity, and appealing mien—becoming literally incarnate in the environment where this witness is given—Christians must communicate to people everywhere what God has done for man in Christ and what he can do in men through Christ, whatever be their record and wherever they live.

The finest definition of evangelism with which I am acquainted was phrased in 1918. It was subsequently adopted and expounded in 1945 by a commission of Anglican churchmen in England and dedicated to Archbishop William Temple, in a book entitled *Towards the Conversion of England*. Its words run thus: "To evangelise is so to present Christ Jesus in the power of the Holy Spirit, that men shall come to put their trust in God through Him, to accept Him as their Saviour, and serve Him as their King in the fellow-ship of His church" (p. 1). But how is this to be accomplished in an effective manner? If people living in a world that is alienated from Christianity are to take the Christian gospel seriously, they must be able to take Christians seriously. Christians who are engaged in the work of evangelism, or who are committed to the cause which professional evangelists represent, must win a right to be heard because of the kind of people they are and the things for which they live. This means that it is an integral part of missionary endeavor, both in so-called "Christian" and in non-Christian countries, that members of the community called the church be known for their moral integrity and their dedicated concern for fellow humans in every facet of their being. Otherwise, this reaction will be inevitable: "I cannot hear what you say, what you are sounds so loudly in my ears."

At a time when unique problems confront the evangelistic task of the Christian church and the church's missionary endeavor in general, there is a sociological fact which calls for rediscovery and fresh emphasis in a spirit of Christian humility. In the context of history and in many sectors of the Third World, members of the community of Christ have played a leading role in matters relating to human welfare in the realms of education, philanthropy, and social concern. This fact, in a revolutionary era such as ours, should inspire Christians and the Christian church in all its branches to confront in the spirit of Christ and under the Lordship of Christ the present-day issues of social and racial justice, whose gravity continues to mount.

Because of the nature of the church as the body of Christ and its functional responsibilities, it is obvious that Christians are also under obligation in their witness to pursue *unity* among themselves and to manifest the spirit and reality of churchly unity before the world. Memorable and uniquely relevant to the Christian situation today are the words which

Jesus prayed on the night before his crucifixion: "I do not pray for these only, but also for those who believe in me through their word, that they may all be one; even as thou, Father, art in me, and I in thee, that they also may be in us, so that the world may believe that thou hast sent me" (John 17:20 f.).

Not only is the import of this famous passage often misinterpreted, but its basic significance is ignored. These facts should be considered. Christian unity is here patterned upon the unity existing between God the Father and God the Son. Its goal is participation by Christ's followers in this unity, that is, to "be in us." It is God's design that the manifestation of this oneness among Christians should act as a stimulus to convince the world that Christ had been sent by God—in other words, that his presence in the world had missionary significance. When Jesus, therefore, after his resurrection, said to his disciples, "As the Father has sent me, even so I send you" (John 20:21), he was emphasizing the fact that unity—in the Godhead, between God and man, and among Christ's followers—has an abiding missionary dimension. No unity can be truly Christian if it is not inspired by a sense of mission and if its basic objectives fail to be the fulfillment of Christ's mission in the world. Christian unity dare never be pursued as an end in itself. It is, and must ever be, unity in mission and for mission. True churchly unity is unity on the road. The church is for the kingdom and must move forward until "The kingdom of the world has become the kingdom of our Lord and of his Christ" (Rev. 11:15).

3. *When Structure Becomes a Churchly Idol*

With this apocalyptic note, we come to a delicate but very crucial phase of our study. As time has rolled on since Pentecost, the Christian church as the community of Christ has become more and more institutionalized. Its outward appearance as an institution has tended to replace its inner reality as a community.

Now let it be quite clear: Organizational structure of some kind is an absolute necessity for the effective functioning of a community. This is equally so, whether the community be local or worldwide. The New Testament Christian community became organized under Apostolic direction. Leaders were chosen, standards were set, guideposts were provided. Organization has marked the life of all Christian churches through the ages, whether they were dissident sects or represented mainline denominations, confessions, and traditions. For purposes of identity and operation, commitment to some form of institutional shape has been written into the constitution of all churches. Leaders are elected by the vote of anonymous "messengers" or by the ballot of Bishops and Patriarchs.

This fact must be faced, however, that in all segments of the church universal, the institutionalizing process became related through the ages to the aspiration of individuals to achieve positions of power. Pride on the part of church leaders, their demonic craving for power, their subtle aspiration to be "like God" in relation to the community of faith, produced the baneful phenomenon of clericalism. But let me not be unfair to Christian ministers. In many instances the dominant role of the clergy in church affairs has been a benediction. In some eras of church history, however, the clergy have spelled disaster for the community of Christ. In certain periods the church ceased to be the "instrument of God's glory" and became the instrument of clerical grandeur. Religious professionals became the church. Community love was changed into institutional obedience, not to Christ, however, but to his representatives. The progressive development of institutionalism has marked Christian history through the ages down to the present. But, today new questions begin to emerge.

Let us glance briefly at the ecclesiastical spectrum. In the

Roman tradition a classical affirmation continues to resound: "Christ founded his organization"—not his community. With the passage of time this organization became Christ's patron, as can be illustrated by numerous artistic symbols. Following the Council of Trent in the sixteenth century, after the church had challenged the real presence of Christ in the common life of Christians, the sense of Christ as a meaningful contemporary reality became progressively lost and to affirm it as did the Spanish mystics was heretical. But Mary, Christ's virgin mother, became a living presence. The substitution of Mary for Christ as a vital reality in everyday living and in the process of history was given culminating expression in the legend of the Virgin's appearance in 1917 to three children on a Portuguese plateau called Fatima.

The symbolism that greets the visitor as he enters the new chapel in this rustic community represents the Holy Trinity placing a crown upon the Virgin's head. This Fatima symbolism of the new Marian cult can mean, theologically speaking, one of two things. It can signify the consecration of the Virgin by the Holy Trinity to be God's representative in the confrontation of historical reality. Or it can mean the consecration of Mary to be the Holy Spirit incarnate in all things pertaining to the life of the Christian church of which she is the "mother." But, however the Virgin of Fatima is interpreted theologically, it is abundantly clear that the present Pontiff of the Roman Catholic communion gives greater status to the Virgin Mother, and to his church's institutional status, than did his saintly predecessor Pope John XXIII. There is evidence that the concept of the Roman Church as Christianity's organizational absolute is growing in high Vatican circles.

At the other institutional extreme, I think of the small Presbyterian denomination in the Scottish Highlands of which I was a member in full communion during my teen-age years. The total constituency of this church, including members, adherents, and children, was never more than some 5,000. Its leaders believed, however, that the Free Presbyterian Church, which rejected relations with any other Christian denomination, was the one true church of Christ in Scotland and in the world. Worship was most austere. Easter services were associated with the Roman Catholic Church, which was regarded as Antichrist. The Westminster Confession of Faith was given the same sanctity as the Bible, and the church refused to sanction the changing of a single word or phrase, or accept any fresh interpretation of its traditional standards. But the church's leaders, both clergy and laity, believed in their denomination's destiny. Said a layman to me in my early youth, "Our church may be despised today, but when the Millennium comes it will be recognized as the one true church!"

Who said "never the twain shall meet"? Here is one of the ironic paradoxes of church history. The point at which Protestant sectarian absolutism and Roman pontifical absolutism can meet is the glorification by each of its own ecclesiastical establishment as the one true church of Jesus Christ. In both these polar extremes, the church ceases to be the servant of Christ and makes Christ the servant of the church. But let me mention another paradox, very different in character. In the small, institutionally conceited and self-centered church establishment to which I have referred, there were men and women in its membership, including my own parents, who were saintly Christian people in the deepest sense. Moreover, at a communion service celebrated on a hillside under the auspices of this denomination Jesus Christ spoke to my boyhood heart and I became his forever. For Christ is not bound by any church structure.

As regards the Roman Catholic Church, revolutionary change is taking place. Jesus Christ is being rediscovered in the great Roman communion. He is being acclaimed in many sectors as a potent reality who acts independently of the institutional church and its hierarchy. So, too, as regards the contemporary reality and work of the Holy Spirit. *Jubilee* (now *U. S. Catholic and Jubilee*), a leading Roman Catholic magazine, recently published an article entitled "Catholic Pentecostalism." This article appeared at a time when at the Catholic grass roots, among clergy and laity alike, silence grows regarding the Virgin and her role in the Church. Coincidentally, following the new spirit of Christian freedom and responsibility introduced into the Roman communion by Pope John XXIII, a spirit intensified and made articulate by the Second Vatican Council, a new challenge is being addressed to Christian institutionalism and the church establishment. But, ironically, in a period when the right of dissent is being increasingly sanctioned within the Roman Catholic Church, which has been history's most institutionalized and arrogant organization, this right is being denied or looked at askance in certain Protestant establishments. What does this signify? Protestantism faces the peril of becoming Romanized at a time when Catholicism is becoming de-Romanized.

4. *The Ecumenical Dilemma*

A second shadow beclouds the Christian community today in its effort to give visible expression to the church's oneness in Christ. That shadow I call *ecumenicalism*. Could anything be more heretical than the fact that one who for decades lived devotedly at the heart of the movement which Archbishop Temple designated as the "great new fact of our time," should seriously question the current direction which the ecumenical movement is taking? My concern, however, is this: The dynamic missionary vision that created the "great new fact" is being replaced by an institutional image which allures leading ecumenists. In consequence, the ecumenical movement tends to be less and less motion outwards and onwards towards frontiers. It becomes instead increasing motion towards the realization of an ordered, ecclesiastical structure. In a subtle manner dedication to mission becomes merely the pursuit of harmony.

Two very delicate questions are the meaning of evangelism and what it signifies to be "a new creation in Christ." Because such basic issues are considered divisive and do not contribute to unity, they are either quietly evaded or they are not pursued to the point of creative controversy. When the Central Committee of the World Council of Churches met in Rolle, Switzerland, in 1951, the following statement was approved by the Committee:

> We would especially draw attention to the recent confusion in the use of the word "ecumenical." It is important to insist that this word, which comes from the Greek word for the whole inhabited earth, is properly used to describe everything that relates to the whole task of the whole Church to bring the Gospel to the whole world. It therefore covers equally the missionary movement and the movement towards unity, and must not be used to describe the latter in contradistinction to the former.

But this precisely is what has happened. Dynamic missionary effort in its full dimension and multiple facets at home and abroad is no longer graced with the designation "ecumenical," although it was this effort that gave birth to the term and also to the movement toward unity. But now unity is not for mission. Unity is for unity. This obsession with unity for its own sake, this movement towards oneness in sentiment and structure with no clear understanding of or commitment to the *task* of a united church locally or in the world, is what I call *ecumenicalism*. This trend I am compelled to challenge as being *appearance* and not reality.

Ecumenical reality is something quite different and should be zealously promoted. It involves an objective and realistic view of man and his world, of Christ, the gospel, and the church, and also of the kingdom of God for which the church exists and must work. In this "ecumenical era," when the world as an "ecumenical organism" (to use phrases of the philosopher Hermann Kyserling) is more physically united and more spiritually divided than at any other time in human history, ecumenically concerned Christians must confront co-operatively the realities of the human situation and be sensi-tive to the challenge they present. At the risk of being charged with the use of journalistic clichés, let the fact be emphasized that we face today not only revolution, but revolution within the revolution. We confront the revolt of youth, violence, nihilism, racial discrimination, impoverished millions upon millions. In the shadow of all this, there is corruption in high places. And in this and other countries is witnessed the re-solve of the sons of Mammon to maintain by force those forms of social order that are responsible for the dereliction of the poor. Christian ecumenists, concerned about the insti-tutional oneness of the church, must therefore face current reality not only in the world but also in the church itself. They must make up their minds as to what the real issues are that confront Christianity today and what the concerns are that should be given top priority. The assumption that the supreme need of the churches is to work towards "becoming one" as a single ecclesiastical structure, must be scrutinized in the perspective of the Bible, history, theology, sociology, and human nature.

Let me become more specific and perhaps more contro-versial. In the spirit and context of the imperative, "Let the church be the church," that gripped my thinking in the twen-ties and caused me to wrestle agonizingly with the dual ques-tion of the "church" and the meaning of "ecumenical," may I make the following observations, and with them bring this phase of our study to a close.

One: In view of the religious nominalism that marks the

lives of the majority of the men and women who have been baptized and confirmed in churches of the Protestant tradition, should not priority be given to a united movement toward spiritual awakening in these churches rather than to a top-level, ecclesiastical effort to merge church denominations and confessions in a single organizational structure?

Two: When Christian unity is equated with institutional oneness and episcopal control, and when both these are regarded as indispensable for real unity, let this not be forgotten. The most unified ecclesiastical structure in Christian history was the Hispanic Catholic Church, which was also the most spiritually sterile and the most disastrously fanatical.

Three: Would it not be wise to consider the fact that in the Roman Catholic Church there are more than 600 orders that do not function under the jurisdiction of the Vatican or of a local bishop, and many of which have had a history of dynamic and creative activity?

Four: Dare the phenomenon be ignored that many of the most dynamic, creative, and cooperative Christian enterprises of our time are being carried on in this nation and around the world by men and women who, while loyal to their own denomination, work in a truly ecumenical spirit with Christians of other denominations to achieve important Christian objectives?

Five: In a time of revolutionary change—when all institutional structures are crumbling in the secular and religious order, when the churches of historical Protestantism are becoming increasingly bureaucraticized, when more and more church members are meeting in cells in an un-ecclesiastical underworld, when the Roman Catholic Church is developing evangelical concern and a deepening sense of what it means to be Christian, when the charismatic movement is growing across all ecclesiastical boundaries—might it not happen that, unless our Protestant churches rediscover dimensions in thought and life that they are losing or disdaining, the Christian future may lie with a reformed Catholicism and a matured Pentecostalism?

Meantime, let members of the body of Christ listen to their divine Head. Let them be filled with the Spirit. Let them take to the road together. Let them as they march meet each issue that emerges in the name, the spirit, and the strength of Christ. And, as pilgrims and crusaders on the way to the kingdom, let them have the assurance that God will reveal to them in his own time the most appropriate structure for the one church, whose chief function it is to be the kingdom's servant.

Chapter V

CHRISTIAN OBEDIENCE

&

ETHICISM

Our study pilgrimage now approaches its close. We have reached the fourth and final facet of Christian reality.

Let me recall the route we have traversed. We have studied Christian conviction about God, spiritual communion with God, and relationships between Christians individually and corporately in the "household of God," the church. Let us now address ourselves to the final phase of our study, *Christian behavior under the direction of God.* We will also give attention to what I call ethicism, by which I mean the idolatry of rules, prescripts, codes, and legalistic clichés that become substitutes for true Christian obedience.

1. *Human Goodness and Subhumanity*

The climactic expression of Christian reality on the road of life is *goodness.* The good life is not confined to what one is or believes; it is essentially what one does and the way and spirit in which one does it. "Truth is in order to goodness." This famous saying, which was phrased in a crucial period of American church history, enshrines a Christian ultimate, or what may be designated *the* Christian ultimate as regards Christian living.

In the Christian religion, goodness is inseparably related to obeying, to following, to being like him who spoke of himself as being "the truth," that is, the concrete personalization of real being, in whom the divine and the human were one. Christ also made clear that to love and obey him was to act like him, and to act like him was to be concerned about and to care for other people. It also meant that Christ's followers should confront the human situation in the light of God's standards for man's behavior, as made manifest in the Law and the Prophets and in his own teaching and example. In this context it is a moving and exciting fact that man's ultimate destiny will be determined by his works, by what he does in life as the proof and fruit of his faith. And, according to Christ, the decisive question that will be raised at the Last Judgment will be whether this one or that one manifested love and compassion for the poor and needy (Matt. 25:31, 46).

We are, therefore, confronted with this question: What does it mean to be a real man, a real human being, a Christian, in terms of one's character and behavior in the secular order? To answer this question, it is necessary to introduce criteria that pass beyond sound theology, genuine piety, and loyal churchmanship. Insight into Christian truth, a personal experience of God, membership in the community of Christ are not enough to make one a *real* Christian. Christians are called to action in the world. Christian action—while indebted to ideas, experiences, and concern for the church, its growth and its witness—is ultimately expressed in obedience to God in the situation that confronts one.

To mention the determinative role of obedience in Christian behavior is to draw attention to the fact that action represents the human spirit's response to something, whether that something be an impulse, an idea, a law, a concern, or an inner voice. What a person obeys reveals the kind of person he is. If the premise is accepted that in order to be truly human it is necessary that one live for something greater than his own ego, a disturbing fact must be faced. A large segment of the world's population are living a subhuman existence. Paradoxical though it may sound, people whose major concern in life is to satisfy their sensual passions are subhuman. There are others, equally subhuman, for whom life is fulfilled only through obedient response to the craving of their personal ego for power and wealth. Both groups are subhuman, though, for different reasons. The members of one group represent enthrallment to their own animal nature; those of the other group, enthrallment to their demonic obsession to be "gods." The former are the creators of moral chaos. The latter are responsible for the dehumanization of millions of people in all parts of the world who are obliged to live in poverty because of a social order controlled by devotees of Mammon and his demonic brood. Mammon, as described in John Milton's famous epic *Paradise Lost,* was—let us ponder the imagery—

> . . . the least erected Spirit that fell
> From heaven, for even in heaven his looks and thoughts
> Were always downward bent, admiring more
> The riches of heaven's pavement, trodden gold,
> Than aught divine or holy else enjoyed
> In vision beatific.

A much derided truth that needs to be rediscovered and proclaimed is this: Boundless sexuality and the glamorous publicity given to it, the boundless acquisition of wealth and the status accorded to the opulent, are marks of subhumanity. This is so, both as regards the people involved in such aberrations and those responsible for their glorification. For not only do such people fail to obey God, they fail, as does "Playboy" philosophy, to take seriously the concept of man and what it means to be truly human.

Let me repeat it. To be truly human in terms of man's cultural tradition at its best, and beyond the frontiers of the specifically Christian, a man must live for something greater than his own self-centered ego. That something may be an idea, a cause, or a person. It can be a philosophy of life, such as inspired men like Plato and Aristotle, Marx and Lenin, and their followers. It may be dedication to a great ideal, the cause of human freedom, for example, in its diverse facets, such as inspired Washington and Jefferson, Abraham Lincoln and Martin Luther King, Jr. Or it may be the fascination of a person, whether that person be Buddha or Mohammed, Mahatma Gandhi, or Jesus Christ. But whether it be idea, cause, or person, their devotees have something to live for, something that gives creative meaning to existence, that develops their potentiality, that arouses concern for others and for the world. Life becomes obedience to a dream, to a system, to a personality. For Christians, life is Christ. In Christ the life of God became manifest. Through Christ the life of man is transformed, and obedience to God in Christ becomes the mandate and norm for Christian living in the world. Whatever the issue that a Christian faces, whatever the work in which he is engaged or the particular situation in which he finds himself, it is his obligation to *obey* the God and Father of Jesus Christ.

2. *The Range and Perplexities of Christian Obedience*

But amid life's complexities, what does obedience to God mean for one who takes God and life seriously and wants to be a *real* man? How can he be a real Christian in the society in which his lot is cast? It is taken for granted, of course, that the person concerned is a member of the church as the community of Christ and that he is committed to the church's promotion of the gospel in the world by word and by deed. But how ought he to live and act as a citizen in the secular order? One who has this concern will find it inspiring to reflect that, if the Bible and biblical Christianity are taken seriously, the living God is active in the secular as well as in the religious order. It is God's desire that in loyalty to him and in concern for the society in which they live and for the Christian image, Christians shall participate in secular life to a degree and in a manner dictated by God's call in the existing situation. God's call to obedience is to be listened to in the context provided by the mandate to love God and other people, by the figure of Jesus Christ, the perfect man, whom Christians are required to imitate, and by the presence of the Holy Spirit who will provide Christians with the light and strength they need to make the right decisions and take the right road. But Christian action is to be taken, not upon a purely legalistic basis nor yet as an effort to answer the question, "What would Jesus do?" While there are timeless principles for human behavior, the source of which is God, there are also changing circumstances and new situations in which God speaks and must be obeyed.

Let me be specific. A Christian, while never ceasing to feel that he is essentially a "pilgrim and stranger," must never be a mere oddity or ceaseless critic. He must never take up a purely negative attitude towards the habits and customs of the society in which he lives and works, whatever or wherever that society be. He must adjust himself in the spirit of Christ to human reality as he finds it in his environment. He must learn what it means to render to Caesar the things that are Caesar's. He must use his talents and such influence as he may have to manifest loving concern for people. He must, in a wise and dedicated spirit, employ whatever power or authority he possesses to shape the policy of his society in the direction of moral integrity and the welfare of all citizens, whatever their race, color, or creed. He must work for social, economic, and political policies that have as their objective, or that would contribute toward, the establishment of human rights for all people. And he must oppose policies that perpetuate, or move towards, the dehumanization of man.

When their country is at war, it is the right and responsibility of Christians, as of all citizens, to follow their consciences in their attitudes toward the existing conflict and toward war in general. Christians cannot, in loyalty to God and in commitment to the lordship of Jesus Christ, accept any governmental edict that would give the state the right in time of war to assume absolute authority over the consciences of citizens, over the organizations of society, or over the right of all members of the national community to know the facts regarding their country's struggle and to enjoy the freedom necessary to give expression, by word or pen, to their own ideas. Historical expressions in recent times of this revolt of the Christian conscience against political efforts to assume absolute authority are the *Declaration of Barmen* in the time of Adolf Hitler, the *Letter to Presbyterians* in the era of Joseph McCarthy, and in the sixties a legion of protests against the war in Vietnam.

At this point a vital question arises. What is a Christian's responsibility when his life is spent not in a democratic country where he enjoys the full rights of citizenship, but in a land where a totalitarian regime is in power and in which his status is similar to that of fellow citizens born in the nation? There have been many instances in which Christian nationals, because of their antipathy to the regime in power and to the social order imposed by it, have left their native land for another. They were not being persecuted, but they were unwilling to live in a type of society which did not meet their liking and their standards and which denied them the freedom that they claimed as a human right. This is a situation in which Christians—in the full light of their faith, sensitive to the centrality of the cross in Christian history, and eager to know and do God's will—must, after agonizing prayer, respond to the voice, "This is the way, walk in it." What "the way" is must be interpreted by the individual Christian, but with this criterion: The clue to the God-appointed way is never self-interest; it is always witness on a hard, rough road. But those who take this road will never find themselves let down. They will increasingly develop the quiet confidence that is breathed in the words of the Hebrew psalmist, "My times are in thy hand" (Ps. 31:15).

When the history of this epoch comes to be written, it will be found that some of the greatest Christians of our time were men and women who did not flee from situations where life was difficult and hard because of the political stance of those in authority. They remained in or returned to countries like Hungary, Czechoslovakia, and Cuba, of which they were citizens. They did so because they believed that the living God of the prophets, the apostles, and martyrs—the God and Father of Jesus Christ—was at work in their native land. They believed that he had work for them to do there and that his Kingdom would come there in due course in mercy and in judgment.

Very significant and inspiring, when studied in this context, is the word addressed by God through Jeremiah to the Hebrew exiles in Babylon. They were to settle down quietly in that pagan city. Said the God of Israel, ". . . seek the welfare of the city where I have sent you into exile, and pray to the LORD on its behalf, for in its welfare you will find your welfare" (Jer. 29:7). At the close of seventy years, they were told, the sovereign God would intervene again in mercy towards Israel and in judgment towards Babylon.

This episode in Israel's history has much to teach Christians in our time who seek to be obedient to God in a human situation where they find it difficult to be at home, where they actually live in Babylonian exile so far as Christian and traditional values are concerned. Yet, they feel that God has a work for them to do just where they are. They are convinced, therefore, that their attitude must always be positive and constructive, not negative and destructive. There are situations in which Christians must accept reality as they find it, and in faith and obedience leave the rest to God, willing to "sing the LORD's song in a foreign land" (Ps. 137:4).

It is ironic, however, that many Christians are caught in a dilemma in countries that glory in their democratic structure and their Christian tradition. Consider, for example, the delicate issues that confront Christians today in business and in government service in the United States. Given the ultimates that at present determine economic policy in certain sectors of the free enterprise system, a person who seeks to be loyal to his conscience and also to the business concern that employs him can be confronted with a painful choice. Christian laymen have shared with me their agonizing quandary: Shall they say things they are required to say, but which they know to be untrue regarding the products of the company they serve? They have two choices. Shall they, in loyalty to truth, their consciences, and their God, refuse to utter falsehoods and commit misdemeanors in the interest of towering dividends for their company and economic security for themselves, and by so doing place themselves in God's hands, taking all the consequences? Or shall they adjust themselves to so-called "reality," accepting as absolute the standards set by that economic monarch—his Royal Highness, the great god Mammon?

In a time like ours, relations with other governments are determined in large measure by what is considered conducive to national self-interest and security. Not infrequently such relations are conducted at the expense of righteousness and truth, which become captives of a power complex. Officials engaged in the conduct of international affairs find themselves often in a difficult and delicate situation. This is a time when Christians who occupy responsible positions in their country's contacts with other countries must give precedence as never before to the timeless absolutes that should govern relationships between peoples, whether the nations involved be friends or foes.

Let me mention two of these absolutes. First, men are so constituted as individuals and as nations, that when they become enemies there can be no prospect of a creative relationship between them except on the basis of face-to-face confrontation. If understanding is to be achieved between hostile nations and a constructive solution is to be found for their mutual alienation, they must talk privately *to* one another, person to person, at the topmost level, and not merely *at* one another or *about* one another through public documents or the press. It is my conviction that had a top-level confrontation taken place at the right moment between China and the United States—as I publicly advocated in 1949 following a prolonged visit to Asia—and also between the United States and Cuba some years later, the human situation in Asia and in the Americas would be very different from what it is today. But in both instances the voices of persons in high places of authority who were responsive to Christian reality—which requires that God's creatures, though enemies, confront one another in serious conversational encounter—were not heard. The God of the prophets was not obeyed. Men were dishonored and humiliated by the failure to be talked to directly. Jesus Christ was betrayed and crucified afresh. In that same decade, there took place another tragic betrayal of Christ. A statesman known as a prominent Christian churchman refused to greet or shake the hand of his Chinese counterpart when the two men were present at a small social gathering in a European city. What happened as a result? The circumvention of a timeless principle. Demonic hate took the place of human courtesy and Christian charity. Loyalty to his government's position should never prevent a statesman from being a gentleman.

The second absolute is this. Christians in a democratic

society, who enjoy the full rights of citizenship and who are free from any obligation to follow the line prescribed by a government or business bureaucracy, must proceed thus. With their consciences illumined by their faith and with sensitivity to the voice of God, they themselves must determine the position they take on controversial matters. On questions of war and peace, social justice and racial equality, human rights and the forgiveness of enemies, all who profess the name of Christ must, in the language of the Apostle Paul, act "in the Lord." In Christ they have their being, their status and their hope in this world, and will continue to have it in the world to come. But their witness and all their efforts on life's road, till traveling days are done, must be "in the Lord." They must take seriously the fact that membership in the body of Christ has meaning only in action, for in the Christian heritage "action is the essence of life as combustion is the essence of flame."

Christian men and women must confront all life's issues and make all life's decisions "in the Lord." This means that to be truly and dynamically Christian, a person must be possessed by Christ in such a way as to be an instrument of his will. To act "in the Lord" is to recognize that personal commitment to Christ is such that he must become the source, the pattern, the inspiration of all living. Out of love and reverence for Christ and imbued with the spirit of "caring" for man in every dimension of his being, which Christ inspires, his followers are called upon to live their lives in the light, love, and power of Christ. Taking advantage of all available knowledge, conducting themselves as responsible citizens, sensitive to the concrete situation in which they find themselves, Christians must decide and act "in the Lord." Should the action they take arouse the ire of government or of fellow citizens and fellow churchmen, or should it prove to be disadvantageous to their personal interests, let them resignedly accept the consequences in loyalty to their consciences.

3. Christian Decision and Secular Prescripts

From behavior that is determined by standards and influences whose focal center is Jesus Christ, we pass on to consider problems of behavior that are not directly related to the example of Christ nor expressive of what it means to be truly Christian in the common life. By *ethicism* I mean ultimate devotion in human behavior to imperatives based upon a code. These imperatives may be prescribed by government or by some powerful group, secular or religious, or they may be imperatives that represent popular and potent prescripts or customs. In every case, law in some form or another, whether enshrined in a code or incarnate in a personality, becomes a divinity. Let me briefly focus attention upon two representative types of ethicism and in doing so bring this study to a close. These two types are *political ethicism* and *theological ethicism*.

By *political ethicism* I mean the prescription of standards for thought and action, which if observed by citizens, will allegedly contribute to public welfare and to national security.

I begin by referring to the free enterprise system which has been to the present moment a creative factor in the economic development of the United States and which continues to enjoy social status and political support. Free enterprise has been regarded as an ultimate right to be granted individuals and corporations. This right continues to be granted even when the procedures followed at home and abroad can be proved to contribute to, or to maintain, the impoverishment and illiteracy of many millions of human beings throughout the globe. This nation, unfortunately, has not interpreted the role of a lucrative and powerful country as involving the obligation not merely to show beneficence to people in need within and beyond the national boundaries but also to work in a sympathetic and constitutional manner towards the creation of basic changes in the social and political structure of countries with which it trades but in which it is impossible for citizens to enjoy a truly human existence.

In nations dependent upon our philanthropy, whose rulers perpetuate the misery of the poor and dispossessed, we have failed to manifest creative concern for change. We have, moreover, on occasion encouraged the defamation of persons, organizations, and countries that in the name or under the influence of "un-American" ideologies or activities, seemed to befriend the underprivileged. In the shadow of what will be known in history as "McCarthyism," negation slogans have resounded that have glorified "Anti-Communism," "Anti-Castroism," "Anti-Maoism." It is not a question of exalting or even of justifying Communism, Castroism, or Maoism. The issue is that the devotees of the great God "Anti" have failed to confront the fact that the founder of the Christian religion and the creator of the American tradition at its best gave centrality to *caring* for people in need, whoever those people were. They also ignore the fact that certain countries and organizations opposed to the free enterprise system have shown profound interest in the problems of the poor.

There are, moreover, wealthy corporations and individuals who have failed to understand the true meaning of freedom. They have demoted the concept of freedom in the realm of thought and escalated it in the realm of business. For any person or system that regards it as normal and views it with unconcern that a man can become a billionaire and live complacently surrounded by impoverished fellow citizens, such as migrant farm laborers, there sounds a prophetic warning: "prepare to meet your God" (Amos 4:12). Principles of human behavior, if they are to have creative and abiding significance, must be determined ultimately not by man's selfish interests, but by concern for people. Any political or economic order that fails to give due status to the needs of the poor and the oppressed will not have stable reality, but only passing appearance. The God of justice stands at the door.

4. *Christian Decision and Religious Prescripts*

By *theological ethicism* I mean standards of behavior that derive from adhesion to ultimates that have a religious origin or from a misinterpretation of biblical Christianity. Friedrich Nietzsche created Superman as a new Christ whose followers had the right and obligation to act in the way considered loyal to their new divinity. This gave birth, some decades later, to the Nazi way of life. Today there are neo-Nietzscheans. Whether or not they recognize their ancestry, they regard man as taking over the ancient role of deity and as having the responsibility to shape society and history in accordance with the concept of the ultimate authority and power of man. God has done his job, so it is alleged. But his day is now over, and he is "dead," asleep, or a simple spectator of the coming kingdom of man. With God out, man is in. And the movement of history, involving the advent and power of technology, will guarantee man's sovereign reign.

Some neo-Nietzscheans there are who give to Christ a continuing but not an ultimate status and authority. They consider themselves to represent "man come of age." While they are grateful for the man, for what he did and for what the memory of him signifies, they regard it as their role to be "Christs" in their own right, successors of the Christ. They are loyal to things for which Christ stood, but they do not regard him as a supernatural reality nor as a living contemporary presence who has significance for Christians in every situation in which they find themselves. While Christ, therefore, becomes more and more popular and is more and more reverenced, he becomes less and less an ever-present reality who speaks, counsels, and guides. His neo-Nietzschean followers venerate his memory. They extol him as "the Man for others." They seek to reproduce his spirit and give present-day relevancy to that for which he stood. But him they "know not." Him they hear not when in a complicated crucial situation, he says today, "This is the way."

In the thought and life of that great Christian, Albert Schweitzer—master scholar, philosopher, and musician, who was also a devoted missionary-doctor—we have another type of theological ethicism which has caused great embarrassment to his friends and admirers. Schweitzer believed that in God's world everything that lives should be given equal right to existence. For him the ultimate imperative that should shape man's attitude towards every living thing was "reverence for life." This means that every type of animal, whatever its species, has the right to live where and how it desires. As this right belongs to bugs and vermin, the Schweitzer hospital and its environs in Lambarene, Africa, became a shocking place both as spectacle and resort; and after the founder's death it was closed.

Ironically also, this unusual man was not interested in bettering the sociological lot, but solely in conserving the physical life, of the African natives. This phase of Schweitzer's thought was closer to Hinduism than to Christianity. It is both ironic and tragic that Hindu theology has almost insuperable problems for the social betterment of a large segment of Indian society. This is so because of the status given to animals and their lifelong inalienable rights. The sanctity of holy cows and monkeys and other creatures takes precedence over the welfare of people.

There are also, however, within the Christian tradition, forms of theological ethicism that derive from a failure of Bible lovers in their interpretation of certain biblical passages to give due status to Christ and the full dimension of Christian obedience. In some periods of history, groups of Christians so absolutized what it means to live "under grace" or in a "dispensational" era, that they regarded themselves exempted from observing standards of behavior associated with man's common life. Many who bear Christ's name live in a manner alien to his spirit and in violation of moral principles derived from the Law, the Prophets, and the Apostles. Regarding themselves as God's favorite people, they live morally above law and idealogically against law, becoming antinomian. The pages of Christian history yesterday and today are stained with the record of proud, presumptuous folk who have lived lives of anarchic freedom, claiming the right to the spoils of the Egyptians. When their nation was at war in the forties, there were Americans of this type who ignored rules and regulations that limited the amount of food and gasoline, for example, that citizens could legitimately obtain day by day. They told deliberate lies and committed illicit acts. Such behavior they justified to themselves on the ground that God had freed them from any responsibility to the existing order, having made them "citizens of a new order."

In the great Iberian tradition, the majority of those, both laity and clergy, who participated in the conquest and control of Latin America grounded their right to behave in the scandalous way they did towards the indigenous population upon the implicit assumption that God had given them the status of being his "chosen people," his "new Messiah." Because of that, they considered themselves entitled to establish their own standards of behavior. It was their right and obligation to stand up, in every circumstance and by every means necessary, for whatever involved Spanish "honor," personal or national. In this way a country and its people tended to become deities. Here is an instance in which Christ and the ultimates of Christian obedience can be replaced by substitutes that originate in the alleged elevation to special status under God of certain periods and peoples in Christian history.

Other phenomena of similar type are to be found in the history of conservative Presbyterianism in the Scottish Highlands. Here legalism—loyalty to law, custom and regional tradition—became ultimate for Christian behavior. Let me be forgiven if once again I become autobiographical. I grew up in a religious atmosphere where any youth who had been approved as a church member was supposed to cease being a soccer player and stop attending all worldly entertainments, whether in the open air or in a concert hall. A theatre was Hell. It was legitimate and proper to study a Shakespearean drama in a book but sinful to see it played on a stage. On the Sabbath Day it was illicit to travel by train or tram car or to do any visiting except to a home or hospital where a friend was sick. If church folk had occasion to hire a bus or taxi for travel to a Sabbath service far from home, payment should be made on some day before or after the ride, but not on the Sabbath Day itself. In anticipation of the First Day of the week, the main meal for that day was prepared, shoes were polished, and males shaved before midnight on Saturday. Yet, paradoxically, it could be quite in order for a preacher, after the Sabbath Day communion service was over, to be served Scotch whisky to his heart's content in the home where he spent the weekend as guest!

Let us move, finally, from the quiet Sabbatarianism and the traditional way of Christian living of a small denomination in the Scottish Highlands to the most controversial ethical frontier in contemporary Christianity. What should a Christian do in a situation or issue which, in the interest of human welfare, would involve his total absorption in a form of activity where recognized standards of behavior are set aside and violence adopted as a legitimate and necessary procedure? Take, for example, the philosophy of revolution associated with the names of the guerrilla Che Guevarra and of

Debray, the young French intellectual who was imprisoned in Bolivia following Guevarra's death. The same issue confronts Negro leaders and other concerned people in the United States. The question is this: If, according to evidence, social justice cannot be achieved by methods currently regarded as legitimate, can violence in some form become licit for social militants as a method to achieve their objective?

What is the answer? Two things need pondering. One: The sovereign God Almighty—the God of Abraham, of the Prophets, and of Jesus Christ, who cares for people—will not tolerate indefinitely a social order, wherever it is, that maintains millions of human beings in a state of dereliction. He may summon a contemporary counterpart of "Nebuchadrezzar the king of Babylon, my servant" to destroy such an order, as he did the iniquitous Jewish order in the time of Jeremiah (Jer. 25:8–14). He will execute judgment on a system that pays him lip service but refuses to share his concern for people and perpetuates injustice.

Two: While the imperative of Christian obedience requires that a follower of Jesus Christ shall not himself choose violence as a means whereby he seeks the achievement of justice, he should, nevertheless, respect the consciences and defend the concerns of fellow Christians who may become personally involved in the promotion of an effort associated with violence but designed to bring an unrighteous social system to an end. Let me be concrete: Christians who take seriously that the God and Father of Jesus Christ is the God of judgment as well as the God of grace and that Christ, the Savior and Lord, is also the judge who will have the last and decisive word in the history and destiny of man, must remember this: Loyalty to God's self-disclosure in Holy Scripture, evangelical commitment to Christ as Savior and Lord, calls not only for the evangelization of man but also for the humanization of the environment in which man's life is lived.

That being so, Christians should respect the conscience and admire the spirit of that young Colombian priest, Camilo Torres, who joined a guerrilla band, and also of those American Catholic missionaries in Guatamala, who ministered to the needs of guerrilla crusaders in that country who were fighting for the cause of an oppressed peasantry.

Worthy also of admiration and understanding are Christians who devotedly minister in the spirit of Christ to people who, due to alcohol, drug addiction, sexual aberrations, gang loyalty, have placed themselves in desperate situations. As the human situation becomes more and more complex and confused, it is only natural that the question that sounds most real and relevant in the ears of dedicated servants of Christ should be "Are you running with me, Jesus?" This question can be taken seriously and the Christian vocation fulfilled if the Christian runner, dedicated to the cause of human well-being on life's road, seeks to introduce each object of his concern to his fellow runner, Jesus Christ. A truly concerned Christian must, in all his endeavors to help people, not merely become absorbed into their human situation; he must also, on the analogy of the Lord's incarnation, become incarnate in their human persons. The incarnational, not merely the absorptional, approach to the problems of people is the Christian and creative approach to their needs.

It is one thing, however, to confront a situation in which people live in a state of dehumanization because of the oppression of others. It is a totally different thing to confront a form of dehumanization in the lives of millions of people whose problem is not poverty and social serfdom, but dedication in the name of freedom to boundless glamor, gluttony, and sexuality. For such people, too, Christians must be loving and creatively concerned. But any ethical code grounded upon the assumption that enthrallment to one's subhuman ego gives man the unchallenged right to be and to do whatever he has the desire, the money, or the power to achieve, must be challenged. Such a code faces social disaster and divine judgment. Let freedom be the freedom by which people are made free through dedication to something greater than their own ego, whatever that ego's dimension. Otherwise, let the partisans of the new freedom listen: "behold, the Judge is standing at the doors" (James 5:9).

This age is a time for realism. It is a time to rediscover Christian reality in all its dimensions, as Being, Encounter, Community, and Action. It is a time, too, to examine in the light of the real, what is unreal and solely appearance.

Above all, it is a time for contemporary man, amid the burdens, illusions, and frustrations that beset him, to listen seriously to the timeless words of the Galilean of Yesterday, Today, and Tomorrow: "Come to me."